To Jan

You hav wonderful friend from day one.

xx

y Sonne

The Church, Who Needs It? We Do!

by Yvonne Bennett
and The Women of Mummies Republic

Clink Street

London | New York

Published by Clink Street Publishing 2021

Copyright © 2021

First edition.

ISBN:
978-1-913568-90-0 - paperback
978-1-913568-91-7 - ebook

Contents

Foreword

Mummies Republic

Mummies Republic is a community group made up of women and their primary school aged children with little or no wider social network. We are a project of the South London Mission (https://southlondonmission.wordpress.com/who-we-are/) and our purpose is to engage with the vulnerable in the community through the provision of services which provide opportunity and support during crisis.

Most of our households are working on low incomes, dependent on foodbanks, experiencing homelessness, overcrowding, domestic abuse, food poverty and anxiety.

Welfare reform in the shape of Universal Credit has negatively compounded the lived experience of low-income single parent families pushing some into poverty. On Tuesday 21st May 2019, two years into the roll out, the community arranged for the difficulties of engaging with Universal Credit, and its impact, to be relayed via a theatrical production in the Palace of Westminster. This was followed by a discussion, giving the women the opportunity to tell of their lived truth to the policymakers.

The hope was that policymakers could move towards making amendments to the Universal Credit system in ways which reflected the needs of those who receive the current benefit. Sadly, the play did not have the desired effect as Brexit put all other parliamentary business on the backburner. The struggle to be heard continues.

Winnie Baffoe
London
March 2020

Acknowledgements

a nod to the people without whom this book would not have been written.

This book was inspired by the community who work, meet and worship in the Bermondsey Central Hall Methodist Church (BCH), in particular Winnie Baffoe and the women of Mummies Republic. I am indebted to this group of women who gave their time and their stories; letting me into their lives, enabling this book to be written.

Life in Britain today has seen an increase in those using foodbanks alongside families falling into rent arrears and facing eviction. Add to this an increase in people being diagnosed with mental health issues, people identifying as being lonely and isolated and the country can appear broken.

The Church also looks to be in crisis as numbers attending continue to fall and those identifying as atheist/agnostic continue to rise. Austerity measures and the implementation of the government's welfare reform system, Universal Credit, has seen, not only less public money being available to run necessary social services but some of the most vulnerable experiencing a drop in their weekly income. There has been an increase in individuals reporting feelings of stress as they attempt to navigate their way through the new benefit system. For those still on the old systems, as they witness friends and family experiencing life on Universal Credit, their fear of what is to come, when this welfare reform program is finally rolled out across the country, is palpable.

The gaps in social provision, through austerity and the government's new welfare reform program are increasingly, being undertaken by local Church organisations. Where there is a need to be met more Church groups appear to be reaching out into their communities. However, it cannot be ignored that, for many, the Church has become an historic institution, one that can appear to hold no relevance in their lives. Religious belief and practice have declined dramatically over the past fifty years. However, if the Church was to become an agent for social wellbeing could it regain its relevance within Britain? Could this a way for the Church to remove itself from special measures? This book explores these questions by looking at the lived religious lives of a group of single mums in South London.

I wish to thank Peter Brierley, of Brierley Consultancy, for meeting with me, giving his time and providing data surrounding the decline of Church attendance in twenty-first-century Britain. Evidence on the usage of foodbanks has been obtained through The Trussell Trust using the research they carried out in collaboration with the University of Oxford and King's College, London. Information was also gathered from The Joseph Rowntree Foundation and Gingerbread.

Cross-party politicians, at both local and national level, have also been helpful in gaining a perspective on how Universal Credit was shaped and implemented. Those approached kindly gave their time to answer my questions and their permission for their answers to be used.

This book has been written to give those most affected by this latest welfare reform a voice, to let them be heard throughout Westminster and beyond. It could not have been written without the stories of those experiencing life on Universal Credit, these include the testimonies of the women of Mummies Republic as well as others from throughout the UK. Including the voices of others show that problems with this welfare reform program are not London-centric.

Introduction

the who, why, what, where and when

This book has come to fruition thanks to my involvement with Mummies Republic and my PhD research into the role of the Church as an agent for social wellbeing. I am using 'Church' to encompass all Christian Churches in Britain today, applying Jessica Rose's definition:

> Christian Churches – Western and Eastern – who profess the Trinity and the incarnation, regard themselves as the Body of Christ, and celebrate the Eucharist. (Rose, 2009, p.2)

From the beginning of this project my aim was to employ an ethnographic methodology; using interviews and observation as means of data collection. I wanted to take a conversation driven approach to this research. As a social researcher I am studying the lived experiences of the participants, therefore, it was important that I establish a relationship with each of them. These relationships are based on trust and transparency. To do so I had to build a rapport with the women, gain their confidence and, importantly, take time. The data has been collected over a period of eighteen months, although my relationship with Mummies Republic spans many years.

Unheard Voices and Lived Religion

Mummies Republic is a group of mothers living in low income households, experiencing poverty and isolation who come together to give and gain support in a religious setting. They encompass a group in which very little in-depth knowledge has been acquired, with regard to lived religion. The term lived religion is described as the ways in which people practice religion in their everyday lives (Hunt 2005; Crawford-Sullivan 2011). This may or may not include worship in a religious setting and can be formal or informal. Crawford-Sullivan questions why this group, mothers living in poverty, and their lived religious lives are unrepresented when it comes to sociological enquiry. As she points out, this requires investigation not least because:

> Such women's lives are difficult and challenging: juggling searches for housing and decent jobs, struggling to care for children, surviving on welfare or working at low-wage service jobs that often lack dignity and benefits, coping with family disruption and perhaps facing physical or mental health problems or addictions. It seems likely that many poor mothers might involve faith in their daily activities and find purpose or meaning through religious faith. (Crawford-Sullivan 2011, p.5)

Research has been carried out in areas such as: single families living in poverty; women and religion; isolation experienced by nuclear families; as well as research into poverty within Black and Minority Ethnic (BAME) groups. As primary research is lacking for this specific cohort of women it is important to examine how this demographic experience life with regard to religious belief and practice; as well as how they have been impacted by the latest welfare reform. The experiences of these women will be examined through an intersectional lens. Although not all who attend the group identify as having a religious faith, the Wednesday meetings have a religious element to them.

I have known Winnie Baffoe and Mummies Republic since its creation in 2012. I came to the group as a volunteer teacher from the now defunct charity Kids Co. I was at that time working with young mothers teaching parenting skills and required a safe space that could accommodate the mothers, their babies and infants. BCH[1] kindly offered the use of their hall and it was here, on Wednesdays, that we met. The seeds were sown for what was to become Mummies Republic. I must add at this point that Winnie is solely responsible for nurturing this group and making it flourish, I can take no credit for this wonderful transformation. The ethos of this group that makes it, in my opinion, inspirational is that it is for mummies by mummies. This group is taking back an element of control over their lives and the lives of their children by asking for help and, when they are able to, giving help and support back to others. Winnie wrote of one incident when a group member offered assistance to one mother when she was in financial difficulty:

> As one mum held our latest victim of Universal Credit, she said 'I have £10 in my purse, can I give that to you?' These are families that often only hold £10–20 for their electric meters. (Winnie 2019)

This was a woman prepared to give money that she could little afford to lose to someone who was in more immediate need. Martela and colleagues point out that 'Research on life aspirations and goals has indeed shown that striving to give to others is beneficial for wellbeing' (Martela et al. 2016, p.751). The impact of giving help to others on mental health wellbeing and the links to lived religion forms part of this research.

Abigail Brooks proposes that researchers 'need to begin with women's lives, as they themselves experience them' (Brooks 2011, p.4). It is through everyday occurrences that women cultivate knowledge, gain skills and make choices. Yet how much choice do these women have over their lives and the lives of their children? For this group of women employment choices are scant. The majority have little or no formal qualifications. Add to this the problems many have over childcare and their

---

1   Bermondsey Central Hall Methodist Church

choices are limited. Yet, within this group, the majority of the women work part-time. Winnie spoke to me of the strong work ethic the mothers hold. Crawford-Sullivan writes of the work ethic of single American mothers as having its roots in the Protestant work ethic. She proposes that 'Poor mothers believe hard and honest work pleases God, even if the jobs are bad' (Crawford-Sullivan 2011, p.71). I discussed this theory with the mothers during a Bible study session.

The Churches

In 2012 the London City Mission[2] commissioned a census into London congregational attendance. They sought to gain an overview into the shape of Church congregational numbers in London. Was it all doom and gloom? Are we, as a nation, witnessing the terminal decline of the Church? The census was carried out by Brierley Consultancy on the 14th October 2012. Data revealed that around 9% of Londoners were at church on that specific day. These figures were encouraging as they showed, since the previous census in 2005, an increase in numbers. This increase was not only in the numbers of those in attendance but also an increase in new Churches being established and patronised. However, as Brierley points out 'the London Church scene is complicated' (Brierley 2013, p.3). What Brierley discovered in London does not equate with the rest of Britain. A survey has shown a decrease of 7% in British Church affiliation in the five years from 2012–2017 (Brierley 2017). Age, denomination, location and the cultural identity of those attending worship requires careful comparison and evaluation with Church data from Britain as a whole. By doing so, the discrepancy between London and the rest of the country can be clarified. I examine such discrepancies in Chapter One.

---

2   The London City Mission is an organisation established over 180 years ago to spread the gospel to the poor of London. Today it works in partnership with other Churches and is involved in Church planting.

The Church as an Agent for Social Wellbeing

The fact that the Church is in decline is not disputed. The reasons behind this decline and ways in which to halt and rebuild continue to be debated. In 2014 Anselm Min posed this question to eight prominent theologians: 'What is the most compelling theological issue today?' (Min, 2014, p.ix). He was furnished with eight different answers. The answers given were published as a series of essays, two of which are of significance to this book. The first is Min's own answer which relates to Christian identity within an increasingly secular society. The second is by Robert Schreiter and his proposal that it is the ways in which the Churches relate to present day societies that will help rebuild relevance. Min and Schreiter both suggest that by the Church reaching out and taking on a more prominent social role it can begin to rebuild its relevance within twenty-first-century society. For Min this means that the Church becomes the agent rather than the agenda in present day societies (Min 2014). Schreiter focuses on poverty and those most in need. He looks at the ways in which those in Church authority must come together to give assistance (Schreiter 2014). Both Min and Schreiter write from the position of American Catholics but I am proposing that their views can be transferred to all Christian denominations in Western societies. Kayleigh Garthwaite's 2016 research into foodbank use in Britain looks at the high prevalence for foodbanks to be situated in and run from church buildings by those with a practicing faith. She notes that:

> The 42000 volunteers who staff Trussell Trust foodbanks every week are predominately practicing Christians who see their voluntary work as part of discipleship and duty in terms of the Gospel of Mark, chapter 25; 35–37' (Garthwaite 2016, p.29)

However, it is imperative that those running such services do so from a position they can sustain both financially and with adequate manpower. They must also be careful not to forget members inside the congregation who may also be in need. There is a risk they can feel alienated and resentful of this philanthropy (Rose 2009).

The Methodist Church has long been associated with holding a social conscience. John Wesley was known to make charitable visits to prisoners and the destitute. He held a conviction that education was the route out of poverty. As such, early Methodists were involved with the foundation of schools for the poor (Tabraham 1995). The importance of education goes back not just to the times of Wesley but to the genesis of the Reformation. Education was a particular preoccupation of John Knox as he believed the road to true Protestantism was to be found in literacy and an ability to read and understand the Bible. For the mothers of Mummies Republic, their children's education is of the utmost importance. One aspect of the Wednesday meetings is an hour, set aside, to help the children with homework and to listen to them read or to sit and read to them.

Many organisations make use of the BCH building. Lunch clubs for the elderly, youth groups, an advice centre, a foodbank and affordable accommodation all operate out of this Methodist Hall. This is a Church which reaches out into its community, to the religious and non-religious of Bermondsey, south London. The Church may appear to be losing significance within British society; however, many people turn to religion when they experience times of crisis (Rose 2009; Crawford-Sullivan 2011). As Crawford-Sullivan points out, 'religion often comes to play a more prominent role in people's lives during times of stress. (Crawford-Sullivan 2011, p.5). In this regard, many Church groups have become increasingly aware of those needing assistance. Many, as mentioned, run foodbanks and offer a safe space for people to talk.

Nathaniel Moody, a Pioneer Baptist minister, living and working in Kent, has established a Church in a major new housing development. He is involved in Church planting and his form of preaching places an emphasis on mental health wellbeing, especially issues surrounding social isolation and addiction. The new housing estate has been created to house the London overspill and is planned to accommodate around 14,000 houses by 2035. It is situated on the HS1 railway line with fast links from Kent into London. One problem surrounding such large developments is that they lack a community history. Few people know each other before moving into the development and many are young families with one or both parents working in London. The developers are keen to foster a community spirit and have built a community centre in which Nathaniel holds his Sunday worship. He emphasised to me that the majority of those who attend worship not only have no Church affiliation but have no family history of Church attendance. This Baptist minister is offering more than just Sunday worship, he is presenting lived religion to a new community of individuals:

> Nobody wanted these houses to be built near them, nobody wants these incomers. We provide a welcome pack for every new household; we make them feel wanted. It's about developing and promoting community. At our worship we have no Christian charges, we do not use Christian idioms. We offer fitness classes, walking groups, book groups and gardening groups. (Nathaniel Moody, 2019)

What is being offered is different from what is on offer in traditional Church worship. For this new Church offering something diverse is having the desired effect of attracting new people. This correlates with Hunt's view that, 'contemporary Christians, in line with non-Christian consumers tend to choose to construct religious identity in an ongoing, dynamic way, from the different offerings now available' (Hunt 2005, p.109).

We live in increasingly nuclear groups where people can become isolated as fewer and fewer of us know our own neighbours and live further from our families. New mass housing estates are built to ease the housing crisis. Families move in as phases are completed, and a new 'community' is born with no sense of history or familiarity. Many of these have little in the way of local shops, pubs, GP surgeries or schools. This new Kent housing estate is a rarity in offering a place of worship. Churches have a role to play in the social, as well as the spiritual, wellbeing of their local communities and it seems that a church, or at the very least a space where people can come together is a necessity.

The Mothers, Poverty and the Church

Mummies Republic meets each Wednesday during term time.[3] Winnie is the first to arrive and begins cooking a meal for all the mothers and their children. The food has been donated by local shops. At around 3pm the mothers and their children start to arrive. Everyone helps out, from laying the table to the making up of food parcels with the remaining food donations, and all the women take a food parcel home.[4] Around 4pm everyone sits around the table; grace is said by one of the mothers and a hot meal is served. After the table has been cleared it is time for homework. The mothers will take a child, helping with homework or listening to the child read. Then 7pm heralds the beginning of Brigade. This is a children's worship and activity session led by members of the BCH congregation.

Research has shown that becoming a parent increases the importance of religion for many single women (Crawford-Sullivan 2011). Many of the mothers I met spoke of their children as being a gift from God. When working with the young mothers at Kids Co. they often spoke of having a new identity, as having a purpose and a family. This new role coupled

---

3   Although Mummies Republic does not meet during school holidays the women can go to BCH to collect food parcels and to get advice on issues that may have arisen.

4   This is a standalone service and is not connected to the foodbank that BCH runs.

with the belief of children being a gift offers one explanation as to why religion has increased importance for this cohort of women. Brigade is open to the wider community; many other children attend this session and it is always well attended. During Brigade, the mothers retire to the main church for Bible Study. This session is also open to the wider community of mothers but, at all the sessions I attended, no other mothers took part. This correlates with Crawford-Sullivan's finding that, 'Although mothers may view religion as unimportant in their own lives, they generally regard it as important in the life of their children' (Crawford-Sullivan 2011, p.113). Only two of the mothers belong to the congregation of BCH, the others have varying degrees of religious affiliation, belief and practice. Bible Study is fluid, usually beginning with a Biblical reading, which is discussed, and ending with a prayer. The middle section is organic, determined by the needs of the women.

Poverty affects around 14.3 million people in Britain, with around 4.6 million of these being children (fullfact.org, September 27th, 2019). Poverty can be measured in different ways and does not necessarily equate to low income. I am defining poverty as when people are unable to afford and therefore provide the basics required for daily life such as food, housing and adequate clothing. Around a quarter of all families in Britain are headed by a single parent (Rabindrakumar 2018). Sumi Rabindrakumar's report for the charity Gingerbread notes that:

> Single parents today are still largely women, with the typical single parent in their 30s. Single parent families are smaller than couple families with children – most have just one or two children. (Rabindrakumar 2018, p.2)

The report also noted that single parents are more likely to come from a BAME background. The majority of the women of Mummies Republic meet all of the above criteria.

Tina Beattie wrote that 'there is still a tendency by those working in the field of religion and gender to elide their own religious contexts' (Beattie 2005, p.65). Beattie's proposition being that, when studying religious practices and beliefs, the researcher is asking participants for honesty and transparency and this must be a two-way street. I am of the opinion that trust can only be built on integrity and to ignore the researcher's own views may lead to an imbalance of power within the researcher–participant relationship. Bearing in mind that this book is examining the role of a female organisation that operates within the confines of a Methodist church I have taken this view on board. My own religious identity is that of, and here I am appropriating Phillip Pullman's phrase, a Christian Atheist.[5] I enjoy church services from the sermons to the hymns and psalms. I enjoy the sense of community and belonging but have no personal faith.

I have also been aware that I do not share the same life experiences of the women I am writing about. I do not come from a BAME background, I am older woman with adult children, I may have experienced periods of financial hardship, but I have never lived in poverty and never experienced periods of crisis as a single mother. Having the prudence to recognise that I am writing this from an outsider perspective helped me navigate my 'other' position. My past experiences and knowledge also gave me the analytical tools which Chang proposes enables researchers to actively interpret their social surroundings (Chang 2008). A large part of my nursing involved listening to people; listening to what was said and to what was omitted. Learning and understanding when to talk and when to remain silent. I also had the backing of Winnie and the women to write this book and tell their lived religious lives. It was because of my outsider position that I wanted the

---

5   Pullman is often referred to as being a new atheist, alongside Christopher Hitchens and Richard Dawkins. Although Pullman has atheist beliefs, he does not denounce Christianity and describes himself in interviews as a 'Church of England Atheist' (Catholic Herald 2017) or a Religious Atheist (Jukes 2014).

women to co-author a chapter, it was paramount that they reinforced this research from the inside.

Welfare Reform

2008 saw the world thrown into financial crisis. Although not as large as the Great Depression of the 1920s and 1930s it was, as Richard Baldwin proposes 'sudden, severe and synchronised' (Baldwin 2013, p.1). The results from this crisis were felt worldwide. In 2010 the new British coalition government, Conservative and Liberal Democrats, set out a program of austerity as a path towards financial stability for the country. From the outset references were made to 'the blitz spirit' and to the whole country 'being in this together' (Raynor 2016). A budget was set which looked at reducing public spending. Over a third of those reductions were welfare related. Austerity is not simply about budget cuts and limited spending. It is also about the effects these cuts have on those who are already in need: 'austerity also has a cultural life, an emotional, affective and atmospheric life' (Raynor 2016, p.27). I propose that, if the largest cuts from the austerity budget were being laid at the door of the welfare system, those who were in most in need were more in it than the rest of us.

In October 2010 the then Secretary of State for Work and Pensions, The Right Honourable Iain Duncan Smith announced the government's latest welfare reform program, Universal Credit. It was heralded by the government as innovative, simplifying the existing benefit systems by placing six legacy benefits and tax credits into one new allowance. It was also designed to encourage people back into work. The government view was that no longer would people be better off on benefits than in employment. The government also claimed that this reform would increase the amount of money allocated to housing, the disabled and those with children. Initial pilot schemes were set up in the North West of England in 2013 with more areas being added to the pilot program over the following two years. The rolling out schedule was designed to have everyone, old and new claimants, on Universal Credit by 2022.[6] This date has been revised many times and, at time of writing, a new date of 2024 has been advised by the government.

This latest welfare reform is not without its problems. The lived experiences of those who claim Universal Credit are poorly related to governmental promises. This new simple system proves difficult to navigate. Money is paid to claimants in arrears, just as those in employment are paid. Yet those in most need do not have surplus funds that would enable them to wait four or five weeks for their first payment. Bills still have to be paid and food placed on the table. To overcome this problem the government has set up a loan system, repayments are deducted from subsequent allowances over a period of several months. This leaves those in most need in debt from the very beginning. The money they are allocated each month does not take into account the loan repayments. This can, for some, be the start of a vicious downward spiral. From the outset, those who take the loan have to prioritise the spending of an already depleted purse of money. Food over rent, bus fares to school or work over the electricity bill? For those who begin their welfare journey in this way, the path out of debt can seem unending.

For people working part-time or on low income, the amount paid to a claimant is calculated on the amount they earned during the preceding calendar month. There is one major problem with this set up. This was explained to me by one of the mothers, Martha.

> I get paid on the 20th of every month and my assessment dates for Universal Credit are from the 19th of one month to the 18th of the next. Now, if the 20th falls on a weekend then I get paid the Friday before. So, some months I get paid on the 18th. So, when they look at

---

6   Information retrieved from https://www.entitledto.co.uk/help/Universal-Credit-Timetable, this webpage has been left online for reference only.

how much I got paid during that assessment period it looks like I've been earning double, so I don't get any benefits. I don't get double benefits next month though cause its back to normal and there is a cap on how much they give you. (Martha, 2019)

In 2019 four women took the Department of Work and Pensions (DWP) to court over this anomaly. The court found in favour of the women. The DWP were refused the right of appeal but were later, following a further petition, given the right to appeal. The next court date was set for May 2020. Until that date Universal Credit continued to operate as before. They released a Commons briefing which said:

The Department for Work and Pensions advises Universal Credit claimants to be prepared for months when they will get an additional payment of wages and budget accordingly or, alternatively, ask their employer to change the date on which they are paid. (Macley et al 2020)[7]

Three of the women, as did Martha, asked their employers to move the payment date to after the assessment period on the months where this anomaly occurred. All employers refused to do so. With the amount of money allocated monthly to each claimant being minimal, I am unsure as to how those affected can plan ahead.

Despite the assertion that more money would be made available for children and housing, this has not been the case. Families are now penalised for having more than two children. The two children element refers to the third or subsequent children born after the 6th April 2017. People are unable to claim Universal Credit for these children unless the child is

---

7   Full report can be downloaded here http://researchbriefings.files.parliament.
    uk/documents/CBP-8501/CBP-8501.pdf

disabled. This has far-reaching consequences for those whose circumstances have changed over the years. This was set up to have people think carefully about whether they could support more than two children. This is, I propose, a clear reaction to poverty porn, a concept that is discussed in Chapter Four. However, as the Child Poverty Action Group points out:

> Even if you were financially able to support three or more children when you had them, the policy will still affect you if your third or subsequent child was born on or after 6 April 2017. (Child Poverty Action Group, 2019, p.147)

Housing has also failed to live up to government marketing as 'pressures on social housing have meant that particularly in London, social housing tenants have been subjected to brutal treatment, involving displacement to towns and cities they neither know nor wish to live in' (Shildrick 2018, p.47). Could this be a case of social cleansing?

Accessing Universal Credit; notifying of a change of circumstance, logging job searches and being notified of interview dates with a case worker are all carried out online. Some of those in most need do not have internet access. They are advised to use computers at a library or advice centre. Interesting advice at a time when councils are having to close libraries due to budget cuts. For those where English is not their first language, the online forms can appear insurmountable.

The Reasons Being

Why then a book about this specific cohort of women's experiences of life navigating their way around a new welfare system? What has this got to do with the Church? Why should this be of interest to the rest of the British public? Little is known about this cohort of women and their lived religious lives during times of austerity. Little is known of the way religion impacts their lives during periods of stress with reference to welfare reform. I propose that the life experiences of those living through the changes brought about by welfare reform are important for the rest of society to acknowledge and understand. We cannot continue to turn a blind eye to those in need around us. The majority of the mothers who make up Mummies Republic work part-time. This in itself brings many challenges, not least the expense of childcare. Many of the mothers are first generation immigrants, from Africa, Latin America and Europe. They come from a variety of cultures and, for some, English is not their first language. This group offers solidarity, and, despite their many cultural differences, they have so much in common.

The Church is in a state of flux. If it is to regain its relevance in Britain it must examine, not only its religious practices but the ways in which individuals situate religion into their daily lived experiences. Religion is not confined to formal Sunday worship. Some Churches are looking at new ways in which they can relate to their communities. This is summed up by the Reverend Deborah Cornish the Presbyter for the Brighton and Hove Methodist Circuit:

> The main focus, to me is about inclusivity… We want to say, 'here is a place that is safe and good for you to be part off, regardless of the God bit. This is just a good place to come and be yourself (Reverend Deborah Cornish, retrieved form methodist.org.uk)

Winnie Baffoe has very much encouraged women into BCH by promoting lived religion. God has not been relegated to the sidelines but is being incorporated into everyday life. For many women experiencing poverty attending worship on a Sunday morning is difficult. There may be travel costs or a perceived stigma for being a single mother. However, lived religion is more than just Sunday worship it encompasses many aspects of life and in ways that, perhaps, are not even noticeable to the women themselves. What they do recognise within the walls of BCH is security, friendship and understanding; a good place to come and be themselves.

Under the guidance and with the encouragement of Winnie Baffoe, Mummies Republic decided to take their stories to those in power, to those who were making the decisions surrounding welfare reform but who were not, themselves, experiencing the problems. They wanted to show the individual behind each claim, they wanted to present the person not the statistic. To do so they began by having their stories expressed in a play to be performed for the politicians in Westminster. The play was written for them by a professional company and performed by professional actors. The play utilised the women's stories; however, the women lacked the confidence to play themselves. They attended the performance and answered questions afterwards. Sadly, due to Brexit and the political upheaval it caused, few were there to watch it. This book aims to give their stories a wider audience.

The Programme from the play that was performed at the Palace of Westminster. The art works in the programme were painted by Susanna MacInnes. Susanna attended a Wednesday session to paint the picture on the front cover. She also visited some of the women at home and painted their portraits and portraits of their children.

The women had three areas they wanted a parliamentary discussion to be held on. The play was to be the catalyst, having those in power discussing the reality of this welfare reform program. Winnie sent out in an email, alongside an invitation to attend the paly, to the then Secretary of State for Work and Pensions. Sadly, the minister declined to attend. The discussion points were met with an email containing departmental answers.

1: A moratorium of sanctions for low income/ single unit families during the summer holidays, with the perspective that after the summer recess Parliament can discuss how to be engage this group in the absence of sanctions.

2: Financial assistance to enable low income/ single unit families to cover child costs during the summer holiday.

3: On return from recess Parliament to discuss the need to enact the socio-economic duty and that UC in its functions should address socio-economic disadvantage.

Email Invitation

My name is Winnie Baffoe and I am Coordinator of a church community group *Mummies Republic*, based in South East London. It is a group made up of women on the margins along with their children of primary age. Some of our members are currently on Universal Credit and many are in work. Together we have helped inform a play to be performed in the Palace of Westminster with professional actors to highlight the women's experiences of accessing Universal Credit.

The short 30-minute play – being shown in the **Jubilee Hall on the 21st May, 7–8pm**, is being supported by the Joseph Rowntree Foundation and hosted by our local

MP Neil Coyle. Our intention is that the play will be followed by a discussion with cross-party MP's such as yourself on how collectively we can help people access Universal Credit in its intended spirit.

The purpose of the evening is not to vent frustration or draw guilt, but to find collective pathways forward to addressing issues such as additional childcare costs during the summer holidays and how best to support those who are struggling to access Universal Credit.

We have spent a lot of emotional time and money harvesting this engagement and we feel it will only work if we have your company – either as a guest, or ideally also as a speaker where we'd be very happy to offer you a keynote platform. As Coordinator of the group I know it will help raise self-esteem within the community and trust in our government if you could come and engage with Mummies Republic at this crucial event.

I look forward to your response.

Winnie Baffoe, Pioneer Minister Methodist Church

CHAPTER 1

The Church in Crisis

from spiritual health to serving spirits

Facts, Figures and Statistics

Britain has a religious pluralistic society with the numbers of those identifying as Christian decreasing whilst those identifying as atheist/agnostic are on the rise. If one is to consider the doom and gloom predictions from the secularisation theorists (Steve Bruce; Talcott Parsons) then, in Britain, more churches will close and take on other uses. Many, in reference to the subtitle of this chapter, will become bars and clubs, such as the Òran Mòr in Glasgow's West End. This bar was formally Kelvinside Parish Church.

The UK Church Statistics No.3: 2018 Edition shows that, between 2012 and 2017, 1737 churches closed their doors. However, these numbers are offset by the opening of 1143 new churches. The figures show that since 2012, the country has been left with a net deficit of 594 churches. The denominations with the most churches opening are Pentecostal and New Churches; those with the greatest deficiency being Anglican and Methodist. In this five-year period the Methodist church saw only one church opening, with 500 closing (Brierley, 2018).

Yet these figures are not UK wide; there are differences when one examines the census statistics from London. The table below shows the increase in number of London churches by denomination from 1979 to 2012.

Denomina-tions	Angli-can	Baptist	Roman Catholic	Inde-pendent	Meth-odist	New Ch'es	Ortho-dox	Pente-costal	URC	Smaller Denom's	Total
1979 Total	982	270	434	276	253	76	31	596	183	249	3,350
1989 Total	987	287	422	292	252	142	51	709	174	243	3,559
1998 Total	991	355	417	264	253	269	79	875	162	197	3,862
2005 Total	1,017	368	411	307	251	253	94	1,005	152	229	4,087
% change 05-12	+1%	-1%	-7%	+12%	-8%	+8%	-16%	+44%	-5%	+117%	+17%
No opened	46	8	0	48	0	26	0	488	0	284	900
No closed	32	11	30	27	4	9	15	43	8	17	196
2012 Total	**1,031**	**365**	**381**	**328**	**231**	**270**	**79**	**1,450**	**144**	**496**	**4,791**
2020E Total	1,037	370	364	351	226	258	84	1,657	136	547	5,030

Table 1.1 Number of London churches by Denomination, 1979-2012 (Brierley 2013, p.23).

London has witnessed 900 new churches open between 2005 and 2012, with 196 closing their doors. This leaves London with a net increase of 704, a sharp variance when compared to the country as a whole. The figures from the Pentecostal denomination make for interesting reading. It has not only the largest number of new churches opining but also the largest number of closures. The number of those opening, at this present time, outweighing the number of closures.[8] I have two suggestions as to why this may be happening. First of all, can this, in some way, be ascribed to modern-day consumerism? Do we see here a continual need for something new? There is a finite number of people who can belong to a church, therefore when a new church opens an older established congregation may lose members and eventually have to close. Or can it be attributed to cultural identity? Brierley points out that 'the Pentecostal increase is almost entirely due to the number of Black Majority Churches (BMCs)' (Brierley 2013, p.25). He goes on to say that the majority of these churches are concentrated in relatively few boroughs such as Lambeth

---

8   The Pentecostal figures in London prop up the new church figures for the rest of the country. If one removes the London Pentecostal figures from the UK statistics the number of new churches would drop to 655.

and Southwark. These are the boroughs where a majority of those of African and Caribbean descent live, the groups most associated with Pentecostalism. New Pentecostal churches may be opening their doors in response to an increase in African and Caribbean demographics in certain London Boroughs. The opening of new churches to accommodate those who have just moved into the boroughs may lead to an overstretching of resources with the result that older churches become less financially viable. I can only offer suggestions as to why the numbers, for both openings and closures, are so high, more research is needed in this area.

The Church and Religion

This section begins by examining what Church means to people in 21st century British society. I then consider the ways in which the Church may take control of its own destiny and begin to rebuild its relevance.

Religion is a word that can be contentious, meaning different things to different people. Linda Woodhead writes that despite much discourse it has shown to be 'impossible to fix on a definition which all – or even a majority – can agree' (Woodhead 2011, p. 121). She makes an interesting point in that the definition of religion is very different from the concept of religion and it is the concept of religion to which I refer in this book. Woodhead puts forward five concepts of religion: as culture, as identity, as relationship, as practice and as power. It is the concepts of religion as culture and as a relationship that most resonate with the women of Mummies Republic; as within any church group, religion is lived, encompassing daily life.

The Church and Culture

In British society today, we have access to multi-belief systems. If a belief system is a way of bringing order to, and making sense of, the world then pluralism could undermine religion, bringing confusion. What is to be believed, what practices should one follow? Anslem Min put forward the proposal that Christianity is in crisis as people no longer know what it means to be a Christian. For Min the most compelling crisis to face Christianity is one of an erosion of identity; Christian identity in a world which is both diverse and pluralistic. Min proposes that within this world Christian identity has undergone a deconstruction and faces an uphill struggle to be restored 'under today's very critical conditions' (Min 2014, p.29). Through my involvement with Mummies Republic and the wider BCH community I am of the view that Christian identity, for this community, has not been deconstructed; it is intertwined with cultural identity.

BCH may not be Pentecostal in denomination, but it is a Black Majority Church and as such I am of the view that the large numbers of those in attendance at Sunday worship is down to religion being a part of their culture. The majority of those who attend BCH are of African descent. Adrian van Klinken writes:

> Christianity is enormously vibrant and is at the heart of the ways in which many Africans – young and old – perceive their identity, construct community, engage the world, and shape the future. (van Klinken 2018, p. 915).

Predictions were made, adds van Klinken, that the end of colonialism would generate the demise of Christianity. It would contribute to the secularisation of society, not only in Africa but the ripples would reach into the migrant communities throughout the Western world. However, this has not been the case. 'African Christianity through a process of migration, mission and expansion contributes to reshaping the face of contemporary world Christianity' (van Klinken 2018, p.918). This correlates with Brierley's data showing an increase in BMCs in London.

A Relationship between the Church and the Community

I propose that religion as a concept of relationship lies at the heart of the Church reaching out into the communities. It is the keystone for it becoming an agent of social wellbeing; offering a physical presence, a known safe space for people to talk. Mummies Republic offers a Talking Therapy space led by a team from the Maudsley Hospital in London.

> Relationships with local communities are essential for mental health services like ours to do our jobs properly. The stigma that is still associated with mental health difficulties is often an obstacle to people receiving the mental health care that they need and deserve. It is also sadly the case that people experiencing the greatest social disadvantage who may need the services the most, will often also be those who find services hardest to access. We know that we can't improve access by simply sitting in our clinics. This is why building partnerships with community groups is so helpful for us, and why we are so grateful for the support of everyone at Mummies Republic. (Dr Janet Wingrove 2018)

Rose examined the Church and the ways it can serve the community socially alongside the manner in which it can foster relationships. She points out that, within Britain, going to church on a Sunday is no longer the norm: 'Church goers find themselves at odds with society' (Rose 2009, p.2). This is in marked contrast to times gone past when 'many people "went to church" as the foundation of religious and social affiliation… situated, geographically speaking, at the centre of community life' (Hunt 2005, p.93). This is no longer the case. Attendance at Sunday worship is no longer the standard, no longer compulsory. There has been a loosening of the relationship ties between church and community. Yet people still belong to a church community. Formal religion may be in decline, people may believe without belonging (Davie 1990), but others still may belong without believing (Mountford 2011; Hayes 2018). As I have mentioned, I identify as a Christian Atheist, one of those people who Mountford proposes 'value the cultural heritage of Christianity' (Mountford 2011, p.1). People attend church for many reasons, each of them personal. I do not regularly attend worship but, when I do, I enjoy the ritual. Religion as a relationship can also help alleviate loneliness by bringing an extended family and community into the lives of those in social isolation. Rose writes that 'for some people it is the social aspect of the church as a community, and in the community that makes it worthwhile' (Rose 2009, p. 34). The majority of the women of Mummies Republic live in isolation with their children; families remain in their home countries, live in other parts of the UK or are estranged from them for many reasons. The importance of the friendship and support they find in the group is paramount (Delanty 2010). Friendship groups are increasingly taking over the support roles once situated within extended family networks. As Delanty explains:

> Since people are more likely not to be living close to their own parents, they must rely on other kinds of support in dealing with the practical aspects relating to childcare, illness and the crises of everyday life. For these problems proximity is important. (Delanty 2010, p.114)

Mummies Republic can be viewed as providing a family-based community in which the women have created a social bond in which 'identity and social usefulness are combined in a high degree of functionality' (Delanty 2010, p.115). For Laura the other women of Mummies Republic have become a family.

> It's just helped me so much. And I've been doing things I just couldn't do before, like I have never been able to go on holiday with the kids because just the thought of doing it on my own. I just could not do it because

I wouldn't know how my mental health would be and I'd panic. Now I've gone away with these guys to Butlins and I coped. It's like a family. These are all like my sisters and it's no matter how bad I'm feeling. (Laura 2018)

Religion has always been a daily part of Laura's life. As a teenager, following childhood abuse, she spoke of sitting outside a church, unable to go in, but praying. This was her safe space, a place to go to when she was unable to cope with past trauma. Laura is one of the mothers who attends Sunday worship at BCH, although she does so infrequently.

There is an aspect of the women's lives which places an emphasis on religion as a relationship and this is in the coming together to eat on a Wednesday afternoon. Day writes about the 'commensal' characteristic of eating together. She explains commensal as being 'the notion of eating together with a particular symbolic value' (Day 2017, p.65). This includes the rituals surrounding the meal, something that I observed every Wednesday. The women have all taken on certain roles. Winnie cooks, Laura serves, Aunty P gets the children to the table and says grace. Grace serves a dual purpose; it not only offers up thanks to God, but it gives a minute of calmness separating the period of busyness and activity before the meal to a period of communion. The Wednesday meals always reminded me of my own family meals when my children were young. Everyone coming together, chatting about their day and listening to others.

The Church as an Agent not an Agenda

Christianity is on the defensive; being mocked for its beliefs, practices and moral standings; with Christians being made to feel as old-fashioned or superstitious (Min 2014). Couple this with a feeling of despondency and Christian identity is plainly in crisis. In common with many issues, much has been debated on what needs to be done to alleviate the situation. Min argues that this is not the answer. It is not **what needs to be done** but more a matter of **who is going to do it**. A major problem, as

I have previously mentioned, is that Christians themselves are unclear of their identity. Add to this a secular society which is individualist, alongside mainstream Churches which have been embroiled in scandal and the problem is compounded. What can be done to stop the chatter? What plan of action can those in the Church authority initiate? The answer: the Church must become the agent rather than the agenda.

Robert Schreiter (2014) holds a different view from Min on the most compelling issue facing Christianity today. Schreiter's main concern is with the ways in which the church related to a world which is undergoing changes due to both globalisation and secularisation. However, his solution is similar to that of Min's, the Church needs to take action, it needs to find the answers to some of today's problems. The world today continues to have problems of understanding and acceptance of others regardless of technology enabling humanity to be better connected globally. It appears that the more we know, the less we understand. Despite the United Nations setting a target for reducing extreme poverty, the gap between the monied few and the impoverished continues to grow. One in thirty-five people at any given time are in a state of migration (Shreiter 2014). Within developed countries, deaths outnumber births, which is leading to a 'sandwich' generation. Add to this, growing unemployment for those under twenty-five, people trafficking, terrorism and global warming, the world can appear broken. Schreiter, however, makes an engaging point: 'Religion plays a more visible role worldwide than it did just twenty years ago' (Schreiter 2014, p.67). With this sentence Schreiber is proposing the aforementioned geo-economic, social and political elements have all have a hand in shaping the world we inhabit, and religion remains a part of it all.

I find myself in agreement when Schreiter suggests that if religion no longer existed there are no secular principles strong enough to replace it, especially after the fall of the Soviet Bloc. Many of the conflicts the world is experiencing today are done so in the name of religion, however, many peace movements flourish under the same banner.[9] As previously mentioned, the Church and other religious groups have taken on social roles, filling the gap caused by austerity and public sector budget cuts. In order to evaluate the ways and extent to which Christianity relates to the modern world, Schreiter focuses on Catholicism. He does so for three reasons: sheer numbers, giving it the widest geographical spread; most unified of Christian denominations; and the Catholic Church's formal international relationships with many countries and organisations, such as the United Nations. However, this is a Church with its own conflicts; on one side, those who believe reform is necessary to make it a world Church and thus a split from the past; and on the other side, those who believe that the way forward is a continuation of the past.

Although Schreiter has focused on the Catholic Church, conflicts can be found within all denominations. The Church of Scotland has seen some congregations leave and join the Free Church of Scotland following the decision to permit the ordination of gay clergy, be they celibate or not. The Church of England continues to witness conflict over the ordination of women priests and bishops. The churches have to change as the world is ever-changing, things are not and cannot be static. Churches must engage with the world if it wishes to remain relevant. Yet if churches are to become an agent for social wellbeing then they must ensure they have the resources, both in terms of manpower and funds. They must understand what such a commitment might entail. Margaret Harris tasks those in individual churches with asking themselves:

> if this is 'something they want to do, or whether it is something they should do in order to fulfil their mission… whether it is a task that its members believe is a worthwhile one for them. (Harris 2002, p.48)

---

9   The Fellowship for Reconciliation is one such Christian pacifist group, based in the UK.

Difficult choices must be made as no church has infinite resources. BCH offers help on many levels, from the practical with foodbanks and accommodation to the spiritual and mental. Yet to do so takes a lot of energy from those on the frontline. I know first-hand, from attending board meetings, just how much time and energy is taken up trying to raise sufficient funds for projects.

Conclusion

Religion is a complex topic. It is more than just a definition. It is lived, felt, feared and dismissed by both believer and non-believer alike. There are many ways in which religion affects and touches the lives of individuals, hence religion must be considered in the broadest of terms. Christian identity does not exist as a single commodity. It has history; history of the individual as well as history of the group. It is constantly interacting with those within the group as well as those on the outside. It is evolving, both eroding and building. It is not constant. With all these components at play it is necessary to look at how Christian identity is being identified and portrayed within today's societies.

In British communities today, many churches have increased their social role as public services have diminished due to austerity measures and budget cuts. Many now run foodbanks, provide facilities where people can obtain debt counselling, have clothes collections and run soup kitchens for the homeless. The Church of England has an app where one can flag up a possible slavery cases at hand carwash sites. More and more the churches appear to be reaching out into the communities where there is a need to be met. This is where the BCH is leading by example. They have seen the need within their community and have reached out offering support, both practical and emotional.

Many churches do this and do it very well. Yet we are all at different times in need of help, and pastoral care, it seems, is too often seen as something done by the

churches only for those outside, or as something done
by the 'healthy' members of the community for others.
(Rose 2009, p.152)

However, the importance of striking the correct balance
between being friendly and overbearing must be pointed out.
People may want to be welcomed into a community but do not
want to feel pressurised into joining. Rose writes, 'You may be
isolated, and this may not be your cup of tea — and you don't
have to stand up and say you believe all this — but you are
welcome anyway' (Rose 2009, p.39). This statement epitomises
Mummies Republic and the hand of friendship that is extended
to all. The women of Mummies Republic come from different
cultures and different faith backgrounds. They are never asked
to explain their beliefs or lack of faith. Prayers and Biblical
discussion do occur but at no point are the women forced to
join in. Yet, whenever I have attended a Wednesday meeting
all have done so freely. The discussions can be quite lively, but
never disrespectful. The following chapter will examine the
thinking behind Universal Credit, the manner in which it is
administered alongside the reality of navigating and then living
on this new welfare system.

CHAPTER 2

Universal Credit

"Computer says NO"

I begin this chapter by declaring that I am not writing this from any personal political standpoint. My analysis and understanding of Universal Credit have come about by speaking to people, those affected by it, those assisting people in need, as well as politicians. Before writing this book, I had no actual understanding of what Universal Credit was, nor, how it was being administered. My level of knowledge being that it was set up to simplify the current benefit system with each person receiving just one benefit as opposed to two or three. It sounded like a common-sense approach to restructuring the complicated benefits system that was in use at the time. I was also aware that it was being trialled before being rolled out across the country and that this 'rolling out' was being delayed due to problems with the system.

I have included a summary of how Universal Credit is administered as it this enabled me to understand the issues the women were experiencing. Without knowledge of the system one cannot form an opinion nor situate the women's realities in it. The following is a summary of the information I have gleamed from the government's own website.[10] Universal Credit is a payment made to help with living costs and is paid monthly in arrears. It replaces six legacy benefits: Child Tax Credit, Housing Benefit, Income Support, Income-based Job

---

10 www.gov.uk/universal-credit.

Seeker's Allowance (JSA), Income-Related Employment and Support Allowance (ESA) and Working Tax Credit.

Those on a low income, or out of work, who are over the age of 18 and under pensionable age are eligible. To qualify the individual, or couple, must have less than £16,000 in savings and be a UK resident. There is a standard allowance and added to that is an extra payment for children, those who have a disability or health problems and rent assistance. The amount given is assessed monthly. There is no limit to the number of hours an individual can work, what they receive depends on how much they earn. For every £1 earnt there is an allowance decrease of 63p. It is paid monthly into either a bank, building society or credit union account and will usually take around four to five weeks for the first payment to be made.

Applications are made online. Individuals will be asked to call the helpline to arrange an interview with a work coach. On applying they need to give payment account details, an email address, National Insurance Number, housing information, details of any income, savings and childcare expenses. They also need to verify their identity online and require proof of identity in the form of a driving license, passport or bank card. As I have already mentioned, in the introduction chapter, they can get an advance on the first payment with repayment of the loan beginning immediately. Those who are deemed fit to work have to meet work-related requirements. These are the number of hours they must spend looking for suitable employment and the number of hours they are expected to work, if offered a job. For those with a child aged from school age to 12 years this amounts to 25 hours per week in employment. Once the child reaches 13 years the hours increase to 35.

This chapter considers why those in most need can struggle to fulfil the aforementioned criteria. If a claimant fails to meet the work-related requirements this results in them being sanctioned. A sanction suspends payments for a designated period of time, or, in some cases, indefinitely, therefore penalising them where it hurts the most — financially. The following is an extract from an email Winnie sent to board members of BCH. It shows the reality of a sanction.

> Last night at our weekly gathering as we were discussing the upcoming play, I witnessed a mother enter into her Universal Credit Account and gain awareness that she had been sanctioned by UC (this means all payments stopped until the issue is rectified, this can take weeks). She had not received any notification of pending action. As reality set in she began to cry, only for her 7-year-old to notice and repeatedly ask 'mummy, mummy what's wrong?' His little face turning from youthful oblivious joy at seeing his mum, to heartfelt concern, his little world disrupted by this distressing sight. (Winnie Baffoe 2019)

That all notifications are sent online had a part to play in this sanction. This is a mother with no internet access. She gains access to the internet at an advice centre, or at Mummies Republic. As she does not visit these daily, or even weekly, a notification is easily missed with dreadful consequences. It was through logging onto her account at a Wednesday session that she became aware of the sanction.

As Universal Credit claimants are subjected to rigid rules it is no wonder that many face sanctions, I must point out that sanctions on those claiming benefits are not new to this latest welfare reform program (Shildrick 2019), sanctions have been used by both Conservative and Labour governments. What is new is the number of rules that one can be sanctioned for breaking. This is intended to ensure that people go back into employment and plays into the hands of those sections of the media, and society, who portray those on benefits as scroungers or work-shy. This portrayal of those receiving benefits is examined further in Chapter Three.

Political Opinion

As this book is not aligned to any political party, politicians from all parties were asked for their views on Universal Credit. I wanted to gain a cross-party perspective as well as an overall view of how Universal Credit was affecting different areas of the country. I asked family and friends to approach their MPs for their views on Universal Credit. I had to use this method as MPs only respond to their constituents as to do otherwise would result in a massive work overload. Of all the MPs contacted only two replied, Tom Tugendhat, my own MP, and Ronnie Cowan, my parents' MP. Their constituencies could not be further removed, both geographically and socioeconomically.

Tom Tugendhat, Conservative MP for Tonbridge and Malling

Mr. Tugendhat kindly allowed me to use his email reply verbatim.

Universal Credit is the most fundamental reform to the welfare state since its creation. It runs on the principle that work is rewarded, and that those who need the support are able to receive it. It will also benefit more people, with 700,000 people receiving on average an extra £285 per month. It will also help and inspire more people to get into work. However, I must also acknowledge that many people have experienced problems with Universal Credit but am pleased that the Government have recognised this and in the Budget 2018, the Chancellor announced a £4.5 billion package for Universal Credit. I think it's got a lot of potential, but we just need to make sure it's absolutely right and pace the role out so that we can manage the impact of transition.

I'm pleased to say that I haven't come across too many problems with Universal Credit in Tonbridge and Malling. It was only rolled out at the end of November to new claimants, so not as many people are claiming on it now as there will likely be in the future, but so far, the ease and simplicity of the benefit seems to be working well for people. (Office of Tom Tugendhat, Member of Parliament for Tonbridge and Malling 2019)

Ronnie Cowan, SNP MP for Inverclyde

Mr. Cowan's office sent press releases and have generously given permission for these to be used. Both press releases are from February 2019.

Ronnie Cowan MP (SNP) has added his concerns to the continuing failures over Universal Credit as the Secretary of State for Work and Pensions admitted the system is forcing people to use foodbanks in order to survive.

The link between Universal Credit and soaring foodbank use has long been disputed by senior Tories at Westminster and Holyrood – but the Work and Pensions Secretary has finally admitted that the policy, which has been plagued with delays, has led to widespread poverty.

Amber Rudd yesterday admitted that: "It is absolutely clear that there were challenges with the initial rollout of universal credit –and the main issue that led to an increase in foodbank use could have been the fact that people had difficulty accessing their money early enough."

Mr Cowan currently has a public petition on Universal Credit which is calling on the UK Government to halt the rollout and fix the many problems. Later this month, he will meet with Alok Sharma MP (Minister for Employment) to discuss the subject further and highlight his constituents' concerns.

MP meets Minister to discuss Universal Credit

> Ronnie Cowan MP (SNP) has today (Wednesday) met with Minister of State for Employment, Alok Sharma MP to discuss Universal Credit and highlight a number of issues around the policy which is affecting Inverclyde constituents.
>
> During the meeting, Mr Cowan mentioned Universal Support which is to be delivered in Inverclyde through East Renfrewshire Citizens Advice Bureau; people receiving four weekly wages means they are missing a UC payment at least once a year; Student loans being classed as income and affecting someone's Universal Credit claim. (Iain Fraser – Office Manager to Ronnie Cowan MP, Member of Parliament for Inverclyde)

Party affiliation aside, I would like to offer two suggestions as to why these MPs have such different views on Universal Credit: firstly, the different socioeconomic demographic of each area and secondly, the length of time Universal Credit has been operating in each constituency. Mr. Tugendhat is the Conservative MP for Tonbridge and Malling; a large constituency in Kent. Although there are areas of deprivation in his constituency there is also affluence. This area is part of the commuter belt for London. Mr. Cowan is the SNP MP for Inverclyde. His constituency includes my hometown Greenock. In 2020 the Scottish Index for Multiple Deprivation[11] named Greenock town centre as the most deprived area in Scotland. Inverclyde was also one of the areas involved in the pilot

---

11 SIMD is a tool for identifying the places in Scotland where people are experiencing disadvantage across different aspects of their lives. SIMD gives a ranking for each small area, or data zone, which shows how deprived that area is compared to other areas. Changes in the rank for one area may be due to other areas becoming more or less deprived. Retrieved from. https://www.gov.scot/news/scottish-index-of-multiple-deprivation-2020/

scheme. Inverclyde has been blighted by high unemployment since the closure of the majority of the shipyards in the late eighties and nineties. Whilst Universal Credit is new to those in Tonbridge and Malling, benefit claimants in Inverclyde have been involved in this welfare reform system since 2016.

Reality

To gain insight into the realities facing Mr Tugendhat and Mr Cowan's constituents I sent out requests on social media[12] asking for the experiences of those on Universal Credit from both areas.

The following is a statement I received, by email, from Louise,[13] a Kent constituent of Mr Tugendhat. Despite Mr Tugendhat's belief that the system is working it is evident from this email that people are experiencing problems outside of London. Louise ran her own business until she became ill and was unable to work.

My experience of Universal Credit started on 6th January 2019. I was working as a self-employed cleaner and was struck down by another episode of depression. I've suffered most of my adult life with this and had a complete meltdown 2 years ago. So, with no option I had to apply for UC as I live alone in a housing association property and have no savings. I was bleary eyed and crying every day and just ticked boxes but didn't really take much in as my concentration was zero. After receiving confirmation of my claim, it was said that it takes 5 weeks to complete the claim and then you will receive one month's money. As you can imagine, in my current mental health state at the time, panic and anxiety set in. How will I pay my bills? How will I pay my rent?

---

12 I posted on local Facebook groups for both areas. These are closed groups to which I belong; Borough Green Pinboard and Gourock.

13 Name has been changed by request of participant.

I'm in a new tenancy so in a probationary period with the housing assoc. So, didn't want to fall behind on my rent. I rang the housing team up who informed me that if I fell behind my rent for 4 weeks or more a first letter of seeking possession would be sent out. But they knew my claim for UC was going through so was told not to worry.... Too Late!!!

I read on the UC site I could get an advance payment which I could pay back monthly. So, I received advance payments totalling £400 so that I could pay £130 rent, so that would keep housing from sending me a threatening letter and I could also pay my direct debits and buy food. On the 16th February I received my first payment of £701 £383.24 of which was to pay my month's rent, minus the £50 to pay back my advance payment, which left me with £267.76 to live on for a month. The March payment came through on the 16th March, but they took £67 off for my repayment so was left with £250 for the month. I put my last £8 in the car to get me to my appointment with Maidstone work coach on Thursday and told her I had no more money. She said I had to go weekly to Tonbridge now to see them as part of my commitment. So, I am due to go the day before my UC is due.

Louise had never applied for benefits before and needed assistance in navigating her way around the application process. The assistance she received from Universal Credit advisors was negligible. Her main concern was paying her rent, her final concern was food. The repayment of the advancement loan left very little for her to live on. However, despite having only £250 to pay for food and bills Louise still had to attend her work coach meetings, to miss these would result in a sanction. The only concession she was given was that her work coach appointments would take place in a town slightly closer to home but with poorer public transport links.

In the meantime, I hadn't seen on the form that I need to apply separately for Council tax benefit. My work coach hadn't gone through any details of my form I had filled in, just took proof of who I was and my sicknote from the doctor. I rang the benefit section of TMBC (Tonbridge and Malling District Council) and told them my situation. They said I might be able to have it backdated to the first day of my claim. TMBC arrange the housing benefit, but no longer sort out the council tax benefit. Under the old system, housing benefit and council tax benefit was all on one form. When you are told that UC is all one benefit it covers everything is a lie. It's easy to miss this as I did. And there's no way of having this double checked so it's basically my own fault. My direct debits are about to start bouncing as I have £5 left to live on. My next payment is due in 13 days. This really isn't a lifestyle choice. I have always worked. Even when my children were little. My depression has suppressed now, and I am due to start a new job on Monday. As you can imagine. They put you in debt from day one of your claim. This system is wrong and completely flawed. I am in this situation due to poor health, not through choice or being lazy. I said to my work coach about my next payment and my new job and she said the system is set up like this as its meant for people who are used to being monthly paid... This is real life. It's tough. (Louise 2019)

What Louise's story highlights is the lack of information given, not only to those applying for Universal Credit, but also by those working within this welfare program. From the outset Universal Credit was heralded as a simpler method of welfare provision with all benefits situated under one canopy yet help with Council Tax is not included. It is one of eleven financial assistance programs that can be applied for. These include cold weather payments alongside school clothing grants and help with funeral costs. These must be applied for separately (Child Poverty Action Group 2019). Universal Credit is designed to get people back into employment and, in Louise's case, it can be argued that it has worked, but at what cost to Louise and her health?

MPs can present a case to the DWP and speak on behalf of a constituent. They cannot, however, overturn a DWP decision, they can only mediate for the claimant. Louise did not approach her MP for assistance. When I spoke to Kelly at Mummies Republic, we discussed getting help from those in positions of authority. It is an avenue that appears to be overlooked or unthought off by those in need:

> Because I had problems with my flat and I didn't know that I could get hold of my local council to get involved. I didn't have a clue. (Kelly 2019)

Kelly lives with her two young daughters in a tower block, similar in construction to Grenfell Tower. When she moved into the flat there was no running water. She was without this basic necessity for over three weeks. Winnie advised Kelly to approach her local councillor for help. It was only with his intervention that the problem was resolved.

Kris lives in Gourock, Inverclyde. He was diagnosed with ADHD five years ago at the age of thirty-five. The following is taken from a series of text messages Kris and I exchanged on 20th March 2020. Kris voiced his frustration with the NHS, the DWP and social services.

> The assessments have been terrible, I have put in complaints all the way to Westminster. All I got was fobbed off with a cut and paste reply for the Minister for Disabled People…. It was a joke. They had me at Foodbanks more than a dozen times with messed up payments, but it is the assessments that is the biggest flaw. No properly trained

staff on the frontline and no communication between the different departments. (Kris 2020)

The following pictures are some of the correspondence Kris has received over the past five years from various governmental departments. This does not include emails, of which, Kris informs me, there have been many.

'This is my last 5 years of life, being labelled a burden by the government.' (Kris 2020)

Kris spoke of his frustration of getting assistance from those in authority. He has written many letters of complaint to the DWP and has had face to face meetings with his MP and MSP.[14] When discussing the replies he has received from the DWP he writes:

---

14 Member of the Scottish Parliament.

I now suffer from anxiety and depression too… it's the irony on every page… imporving lives… they try to sell you, that's what they are trying to do… it's all pointless. (Kris 2020)

Kris is the only person interviewed who had sought help from his MP. Unfortunatly this had not resolved Kris's problems and he remains unable to work due to stress. Garthwaite notes that 'for people with mental health problems, the government's flagship back-to-work scheme, the Work Programme, made their distress worse in 83% of cases' (Garthwaite 2016, p. 132). Navigating the system can add to stress and anxiety (Garthwite 2016).

The government have accepted that there have been problems with the system, hence the delay in rolling it out across the country for both new and old claimants alike. The following quote from the then Works and Pensions Secretary, Amber Rudd, was included in a press release from the offices of Ronnie Cowan.

Amber Rudd yesterday admitted that: 'It is absolutely clear that there were challenges with the initial rollout of universal credit –and the main issue that led to an increase in foodbank use could have been the fact that people had difficulty accessing their money early enough.' (Iain Fraser – Office Manager to Ronnie Cowan MP, Member of Parliament for Inverclyde, 12th February 2019)

However, as we have seen, when issues such as those surrounding assessment dates have been brought to the attention of the DWP, the reaction has been to thwart those raising concerns. This leaves them with no other option than to take the DWP to court. When the court has found in the plaintiff's favour the DWP immediately lodge an appeal, thus the problems remain.

The lack of personal interaction has been of major concern to the women of Mummies Republic. Martha admitted that she had been lucky in obtaining a direct phone number for a Universal Credit advisor. This was not her assigned work coach but someone in another office who knew her case and was offering assistance. As Martha pointed out:

> I just will not give up; the poor guy must get fed up listening to me. I keep telling him I don't know what I will do if you leave. He has been a blessing from God. (Martha 2019)

Martha knew that by having this number and the ability to talk to someone who, over time, she had built a relationship with and who knew her circumstances, gave her an advantage. Research carried out in 2019 by Peter Dwyer found that when people were having difficulties which required them to contact the Universal Credit helpline that speaking to a stranger and having to recount personal circumstances added to levels of anxiety. Dwyer noted, 'how difficult it was at an often already stressful period in their lives, to talk to over the phone to a UC advisor they had never met before about often personal and sensitive topics' (Dwyer 2019, p.25). For Martha, just having someone listen was important. She was made to feel worthwhile as she became a person, not just a statistic. So often the women get a "Computer says no" answer; their problems assigned to an algorithm by someone they have never and will never meet.

Research has shown that those living in poverty are more likely to be disenfranchised politically. Garthwaite points out that 'People who said they were struggling on their current income were more than twice as likely to take little or no interest in politics as compared to those who claimed to be really comfortable' (Garthwaite 2016, p.70). However, within the walls of BCH, Winnie was informing the women of the ways in which they could take political action; ask councillors and MPs for help and take their stories, through the medium of drama, to those who held power in the corridors of Westminster.

In November 2019, two weeks before the General Election, I spoke to the women about the political turmoil that the country appeared to be in. The country was divided over Brexit and little else appeared to be being debated in parliament. What was interesting was that many of the women spoke of their intention to vote Conservative. Auntie P led the discussion and explained that she 'feared' a Labour government under Jeremy Corbyn. For Auntie P and the other women, a government led by Corbyn in their opinion, would encourage people not to work. For these women of African descent, there is, as Winnie explained to me, a strong Protestant work ethic This corelates with Crawford-Sullivan's findings: 'Mothers connected religion with the morality of work by emphasising the responsibility to work' (Crawford-Sullivan 2011, p.70). Auntie P spoke of her time on a painting and decorating course where a young student was being disruptive:

> I was getting fed up with this, every day acting the fool, turning up late, not doing his work. So, one day I decided to sort it. I made two lunches and I told him to sit with me and eat. I knew he was a good boy, he just never had anyone teach him the right ways, never had anyone explain consequences, show him the ways to work and take pride. I told him he had to do something with his life, and this was a good chance he was being given. He had never had anyone teach him the ways of life, never had anyone cook for him and eat with him. Every time after that when he started, I would just look at him, gave him the look and he would say 'Sorry auntie.' He was a good boy. (Auntie P 2019)

Limited childcare meant that she could not take up painting and decorating jobs, but she now works as a cleaner, for Fresh Expressions.

Unprecedented Events

As I write this chapter,[15] the coronavirus pandemic has reached into every corner of the world. In the UK, the government has declared a three-week lockdown in an attempt to slow transmission. Only those who cannot work from home and whose jobs have been designated as essential may go out to work. Many companies have had to furlough their employees and the future for companies, both large and small, looks uncertain. The government has set up the Coronavirus Job Retention Scheme, which allows employers to claim 80% of furloughed employees wages up to £2500 a month (**www.gov.uk**). However, this will not cover all of those who will be affected by the lockdown, nor will it cover the self-employed. There is a separate scheme set up for those who are self-employed but to access this you must have posted business accounts for the past tax year. As a result of all the uncertainty it has been reported in the Guardian that as of April 1st, 2020 around 950,000 people applied for Universal Credit since the lockdown was announced on March 23rd 2020. This is a weekly rise off over 500% (the Guardian. com, 1st April 2020).

In response to coronavirus, the DWP have had to increase the number of civil servants working within the department for Universal Credit. For those already on the system, all work-related obligations have been suspended, as have all appointments with work coaches or disability assessments (**www.gov.uk**). Time will tell if the system can cope with such an unprecedented surge.

---

15 I am writing this chapter the week beginning the 30th March 2020. We have entered week two of a country wide lockdown and life is looking very different.

CHAPTER 3

Foodbanks

reaching out in a time of need

Foodbanks are a relatively new service in Britain with the first one being set up by the Trussell Trust in 2000. Since the austerity budget in 2010, Britain has witnessed a dramatic increase in both the number in operation and the number of people using them. The Trussell Trust is the main provider, supporting over 1200 foodbanks throughout the country:

> In the UK, more than 14 million people are living in poverty – including 4.5 million children. We support more than 1,200 foodbank centres in the UK to provide a minimum of three days' nutritionally balanced emergency food to people who have been referred in crisis, as well as support to help people resolve the crises they face. Between April 2018 and March 2019, foodbanks in our network provided a record 1.6 million food supplies to people in crisis, a 19% increase on the previous year. (**https://www.trusselltrust.org/what-we-do/**)

That foodbanks are a sad reflection on modern day British society is not in dispute. What needs to be examined is the attitudes to foodbanks, both by those who use them and the wider public. Is there a sense of shame for the clients? Has Britain become reduced to a society where those most at need are viewed as 'other', believed to have contributed to their own crisis through poor choices?

Research has revealed that many people in Britain view those in poverty as a result of austerity as being in some way to blame for their situation (Garthwaite 2016; Raynor 2016; Shildrick 2016). It is, therefore, no surprise that many people who find themselves using foodbanks feel a sense of embarrassment, shamed by those who are lucky enough not to be experiencing food poverty. Shaming is used to regulate conduct. It stands without authority, reinforcing behaviours over which formal law has no jurisdiction. This sense of shame and stigmatisation has been alluded to by the women of Mummies Republic. Stigma differs from, and can be the cause of, shaming, referring to 'an attribute that is deeply discrediting' (Goffman 2009, p.13). Stigmatisation arises during periods of socialisation and is used as a means for the categorisation of people (Goffman 2009).

As single mothers the women have greatest contact with other women when at the school gate, doctors' surgeries and children's health clinics. Bonnie Morris points out that as women, 'We too often employ the historically white, Christian, male tactics of ostracism and shaming' as a means of gaining a measure of power over other women (Morris 1999: 201). Shaming is utilised in different areas of life and analysed in different fields of research; Elizabeth Rosenblatt (2013) writes about shaming in the discipline of Law; Bonnie Morris (1992) discusses shame in the field of Women's Studies. It is a tool that girls begin to use at preteen age in the school playground, and it follows us into adulthood (Currie et al. 2007; Wiseman 2003). Elizabeth Rosenblatt writes that there may be many reasons behind the use of such a device:

> 'Shaming may have many motivations, including a desire to impose norms on another, to trigger someone else's shame, or to inflict reputation-based punishment. Regardless of the motivation, shaming appeals to community norms and attempts to impose them on someone else.' (Rosenblatt 2013, p.8)

The stigmatisation of people receiving Universal Credit has been pushed forward by the rhetoric from the government as well as by sections of the media. Raynor writes of:

> a genre of 'austerity nostalgia', that infuses government discourse, television programming, fashion, branding and so on. This evokes a post-war period and in doing so exemplifies a longing for security and stability in hard times. (Raynor 2016, p.25)

This 'Blitz spirit' and a feeling of all pulling together finds great weight within London and the major cities. The government's rhetoric was used 'both to legitimate the cuts and reforms to welfare and to evoke the kind of disciplining and taking control' (Raynor 2016, p.27). This was picked up by the media in both print and television. From the Channel 4 series *Benefits Street* to *The Jeremy Kyle Show*, those receiving welfare assistance are depicted as being lazy, uneducated and undeserving. Garthwaite refers to the media portrayal of those in need as being work-shy, or not helping themselves as 'poverty porn' (Garthwaite 2016: 137). This media portrayal has led to othering; the result being that those most affected by austerity receive little or no sympathy from the rest of society. Interestingly, Garthwaite's research also found that this 'othering' occurred with those using foodbanks. Clients would label other clients as unworthy of help; these would include addicts and migrants (Garthwaite 2016; Raynor 2016; Shildrick 2018).

This perception of foodbank clients has begun to change as the media has started to report that some people in employment – most notably those who worked in frontline services such as nurses and paramedics – have also been driven to seek assistance, having found themselves living in food poverty. In March 2020, the journalist Chris Valance produced a short documentary for *BBC News*, titled 'We discuss foodbanks at school gates like it's normal' (Valance March 2020). Valance interviewed people working in a foodbank and was told that clients came from a wide variety of backgrounds.

> I've spoken to a nurse, a student librarian, former academic researchers, someone who gets ambulances ready to answer calls, a nursery teacher, a former primary school teacher, a funeral director, carers, a charity worker, someone on a zero hours contract, a former chef, a painter and decorator, the recently destitute, the recently separated, the mentally ill, the physically ill and the homeless. (Valance March 2020)

The facts surrounding these stories are difficult to establish, but, the Trussell Trust's figures show that around 15% of households using foodbanks have at least one adult in employment (Sosenko et al. 2019). This data does not state what types of employment, nor whether full or part time. What the data from The Trussell Trust does reveal is that single parent families make up a large percentage of their clientele at just under 25%, with the majority of these single parents being mothers (Sosenko et al 2019). Greater London has the largest concentration of foodbanks, with research data showing:

> UC [Universal Credit] claimants were two-and-a-half times more likely to be in the sample of foodbank users than would be expected on the basis of their overall number of claimants. (Sosenko et al. 2019, p.55)

The government contested that the increase in foodbank usage is in direct correlation to the increase in Universal Credit claimants. However, in February 2019 the former work and pensions secretary, Amber Rudd MP, was reported as saying, 'Universal Credit was likely to be the main cause for claimants seeking emergency food aid' (Bulman 19th September 2019, independent.co.uk).

Austerity affects many parts of people's lives. It is not just the physical pain of hunger or cold, but it has an impact on mental wellbeing. Thanks to welfare reform, people are living in poverty and, as a result, 'suffer stress and guilt at being unable to meet their own and their children's basic needs' (Shildrick 2018, p.44). The safety net of free school meals for children can also lead to negative feelings of shame. The stigma can affect the children; it 'makes those in receipt of them [free school meals] readily identifiable and thus at risk of being bullied and stigmatised' (Shildrick 2018, p.50). Living in poverty damages childhoods, yet in 2015 the then Work and Pensions Secretary Iain Duncan Smith MP scrapped the child poverty target and changed the manner in which child poverty would be measured. It now focusses on educational achievement and worklessness families. This ignores children living in poverty in low income households, such as the children of Mummies Republic.

Some of the women do make use of the foodbank run by the Trussell Trust at BCH. To do so they must be referred by a charity or a statutory body who have a relationship with people in financial crisis. These include Citizens Advice,[16] local councils, schools, job centres or health visitors. The foodbank at BCH has over 400 referral agents on its database. The foodbank distributes around 130 food parcels a week.[17] There is a limit on the number of times an individual can be referred, although for the most vulnerable, discretion is employed. At the Wednesday meetings the women all take home a food parcel. This is not in any way connected to the foodbank that is run at the church. The women do not need to have a voucher nor are they limited to the number of times they can have a parcel. There is no stigma involved.

Food poverty affects so many aspects of peoples' lives. As Garthwaite notes, 'food insecurity has serious adverse consequences for the mental, physical and social health of adults and children alike' (Garthwaite 2015, p.116). Suicide rates are increasing in Britain. Research by Samaritans has shown a link between those experiencing poverty and suicide:

---

16 Citizens Advice is an independent charitable orginisation which gives free information and advice to individuals on finance, legal and consumer problems.

17 During the first weeks of the 2020 lockdown, referrals increased by 500%.

'areas of higher socioeconomic deprivation tend to have higher rates of suicide' (2017, p.5). It has been reported that 'those in the poorest communities are ten times more likely to commit suicide than those in affluent areas' (Garthwaite 2015, p.133). However, attending or volunteering at a foodbank may hold some benefits for those with mental health problems. For some, they are given the opportunity to have a chat with others, to talk about their problems and be given advice.[18]

Lockdown

As the pandemic lockdown entered its ninth week, Winnie reached out to the women. She had managed to secure funding in the form of food vouchers for a well-known supermarket chain. She had been concerned that, as time went on, the women would be facing increased hardship. Children were no longer at school; therefore, they were not receiving school meals. The heating was now on more during the day, so money was having to be set aside to meet the higher than usual bills. The government had allocated vouchers for those children receiving free school meals, but these were not covering all the extra food expenses. There was also a problem with some of the voucher barcodes being faulty, which meant they were rejected at the till. The women were no longer receiving a food parcel at the Wednesday meeting. The following messages show how much the women needed the extra support.

> I need it is because I am not working at the moment. The children are at home with me due to lockdown. The benefit I am receiving is not enough. (Jana)

> Morning sister, I really need the vouchers to get some food. Thank you and God bless you.[19] (Blanca)

---

18 See Laura's story in Chapter 5.

19 Throughout the pandemic, the need for prayer and blessings was evident through WhatsApp messages. This is examined fully in Chapter 6.

I need some at the moment as I'm not working. Things are really expensive, and I need it for food. (Pat)

Winnie also signposted the women to an emergency support scheme set up by Southwark council.

The pandemic has seen many people experience food poverty as many were furloughed, lost their jobs or, as self-employed, fell through the gaps in government provision. My own town of Sevenoaks saw a new community group come together to help those in isolation with shopping, prescription deliveries and even dog walking. As the weeks progressed, this new group recognised a need for those experiencing food poverty. As mentioned in Chapter 2, this is an affluent area where there are pockets of deprivation. The organiser of the group explained that many of those who found themselves requiring help with food provision had never envisaged being in such a situation, but as the lockdown continued, they found themselves unable to buy food. The following is from Claire Ritchie, a Sevenoaks resident who set up the community group:

They began to find themselves living hand to mouth. They may appear to earn a good salary but with living expenses in the town being high they had little or no savings as they spent 100% of what they earned just on living day to day.

Sadly, the local foodbank did not work for them. Many were embarrassed by the stigma of having to ask for help. To be eligible for the foodbank they had to earn less than a certain amount, had to agree to financial guidance and would only be given 4 weeks' worth of assistance. For many of the families they earned too much, it didn't matter that they were now furloughed so had a drop-in salary or were self-employed and therefore not earning and waiting for the government's assistance. Some had applied for Universal Credit so were having to wait for that to be processed. They did not need financial guidance as, before the pandemic, they were more than able to budget and provide. The foodbank was also only open one day a week and for one hour. They could not cope with the increase in demand.

The new service works differently from the foodbank. People apply online and, if approved, are sent an email with a shopping list. Each family gets £25-worth of groceries a week. They choose what they want, and a volunteer does the shop and drops it off for them. At present we have around 130 families we are helping but this may increase as we are about to do a leaflet drop throughout the entire area signposting our service. (Claire Ritchie 2020)

This group has removed the stigma for those needing help. They have decided to limit the criteria needed to get assistance. They agree this may lead to some abuse of the system. They made this decision as they felt they wanted to reach as many families in need as possible without making them jump through hoops to prove their eligibility. They wanted to give the families back their dignity and remove the anxiety.

Conclusion

Food poverty affects all aspects of life, from the physical pain of hunger to the anxiety over trying to provide. That foodbanks are increasing in numbers with more and more people requiring assistance can be linked to the rolling out of Universal Credit. The shame and stigmatisation of those using foodbanks permeates our media, increasing the perception of those in need being in some way responsible for their own crises. Shame should not be placed on those who need help, rather it should be placed on society who have 'othered' those in need.

CHAPTER 4

The stories from the women of Mummies Republic
life as we know it on Universal Credit

It is important to give the women a voice, to let them tell of their experiences using their own words. Research has shown that mental health can be boosted by telling personal accounts of their lives, by being heard (Rankin 2012; Hamby 2013). As I mentioned in the introduction, this is a specific cohort of women on whom little has been written about with regards to lived religion during periods of austerity and welfare reform. It was important to the women of Mummies Republic that they take back an element of control in their lives by speaking out and by being heard. The women's voices will be heard over the next three chapters, this one will examine problems experienced with Universal Credit; in Chapter 5 the women will discuss mental health issues and Chapter 6 will contain the blog we started during the coronavirus lockdown. This blog was set up to let the women share their feelings and views during the lockdown. It also includes stories from the primary school-aged children.

The next three chapters show how important religion is in the lives of the women. Crawford-Sullivan writes that, during her research into lived religion of American mothers living in poverty, she saw 'how prayer and religious beliefs played a defining role in their daily lives, although organized religion often played little or no part' (Crawford-Sullivan 2011, p.3). This resonates with the women of Mummies Republic. Very few attend churches on a regular basis. Organised religion is not a feature for the majority of the women and their children, yet prayer remains their sacred canopy in times of need. Interestingly, the prayers used in the WhatsApp group were a mixture of conversational prayer alongside quotes from the Scriptures. These were used as a means of connecting with God and as way of offering support to others in the group. These prayers were all that could be offered up during the lockdown as a means of showing solidarity and friendship,

> Dear loving Lord,
>
> As Yvonne's Dad and family goes through this difficult time, please make their time as less painful and show them the way that in darkness, you are the light that will never burn out!
>
> In Jesus's name, your will be done 🙏🙏🙏 x (Martha 17th April 2020)

As the women navigate through the difficulties they experience with Universal Credit, informal religious practice takes on a pivotal role in their lives.

This latest welfare reform program has changed the ways in which the women manage their finances. The majority are now struggling to pay for childcare and food as they move from the old system to the new. Their concerns and problems have been disregarded by the computer programs and a seeming lack of understanding by faceless advisors. I must add at this juncture that the advisors are hindered by the computer systems. No longer can they make individual decisions. The computer does indeed "say no."

The Stories

I begin with Winnie, the founder and driving force behind Mummies Republic. Her husband Peter is also involved at

BCH, running, amongst many other things, the Brigade sessions. Peter has been attending BCH since he was a babe in arms. Winnie and Peter have three young children who all attend the Wednesday sessions. Winnie speaks of the different aspects of support BCH gives to the women; from advice on housing to holidays with the children.

Winnie's Story

The community group was born out of the intention to work with the most marginalised in the community and enable them to encounter Christ through experience of prevenient grace. I gained an awareness of this need when I had my first child at a young age, and this therefore, marginalised me. I, like many new mums had to find my new place in the world.

Initially the focus of creating a fresh expression of church was to engage the first and second generation of young Africans leaving the Methodist Church. As a new mother my social pattern was very different to the latter constituent group and therefore I had much in common with new mothers than young people. Mummies Republic was therefore born out a new friendship circle of mothers within the Southwark and Deptford Circuit. Referrals initially came from the foodbank, therefore there was the obvious food need. On engagement it became apparent that housing and welfare were big issues, so a collaboration ensued between the South London Mission and Mummies Republic. South London Mission permitted the use of their Housing and Welfare officer. Over a period of six months the mothers' most immediate needs were resolved, however low income, food poverty and insufficient housing remained constant issues.

As the children grew the problems for the mothers changed to an inaccessibility to employment due to an absence of work–life balance. The government's fifteen hours allowance for nursery provision was also insufficient. For some, where possible, I was able to secure free childcare, for others work experience opportunities. One desperate Wednesday evening we decided to create a workers' cooperative and set up a cleaning company. English as a second language and lack of time and skill had prevented the mothers from doing this themselves, but, as coordinator, under the auspices of the South London Mission we created Fresh Start Cleaning. We chose this as most of the women were engaged in this activity and it would serve as a steppingstone to wider employment. Hours were set around the school run 9:30–14:30, the London Living Wage and employee rights such as sick and holiday entitlement.

One of the sister churches in the circuit had an opportunity to hire a cleaner. Minister David Hardman was very supportive and paved the way for the committee in charge of the employment process, to consider beyond cost-cutting measures and best value, and to think of the missional opportunities. What was there to lose? On receiving notification that they had appointed another organisation I was angry and baffled. As a church — a body of people which should reflect an understanding of Jesus' upside Kingdom – what reason could one possibly have to deny this post? Why was the tender process a reflection of government procurement procedure as opposed to a local tender for a cleaning post? These unnecessary barriers illustrated the disconnect between Sunday service and everyday life. I, along with Rev Hardman, felt outraged.

Out of solidarity, the South London Mission enabled a post which for which we applied, and were successful in securing, and we now have one member employed under FSC.[20] One could see that the new income was helpful on some levels, however the complexities of Universal Credit hindered any real social mobility and financial stability for the household.

Housing is a major problem for our women, with affordable housing in London being in short supply. We had a family where a husband and wife had to find separate accommodation because the cost of housing was too much. Mother and daughter resided

---

20 Fresh Start Cleaning

in a bedsit and dad in a single room. The accommodation that mother and daughter resided in was substandard. The South London Mission Housing Officer informed Environmental Health at the council and their response was that they had not seen depravity like that in a long time. The landlord was taking over £1000 a month in rent which was covered by housing benefit. The client was advised by the council to pursue eviction from the courts. The landlord also had a list of necessary repairs and amendments to the premises. At first there was an attempt to shoulder the costs on to the tenant, then there were the delays by the landlord. In the meantime, the language and process of eviction was overbearing. A week before the courts granted eviction our client disappeared. Three weeks later she contacted me to let me know she was overseas and was going to see how life would work out back home as she had experienced chronic depression. Her child is British and speaking her mother's native tongue in the classroom was different, therefore her daughter felt homesick. Living with one's parents again, mum felt stifled and undermined. Her husband had also returned to his country of origin. Their marriage was over.

Luckily for them, one last kiss goodbye ushered in a new arrival and so they had to try and make things work. Mum joined dad in his country, however unemployment rates limited access to work. The family returned to London and to Universal Credit. Our client returned to Southbank University, the daughter to a local school and the baby to a local nursery, all of which circumvent our South London Mission's locality. However, as a mum and a student, she is excluded from receiving housing benefit under Universal Credit and prior to becoming a student the cost of their new property, again £1000+, was not covered by the new welfare system. The family has moved out of the locality to Morden, just inside the M25[21] as there are landlords who still accept housing benefit because it covers their rates. Their engagement has been patchy. By all reports the baby

---

21 The M25 is the motorway which encircles Greater London.

is often unwell and the nursery will not accept a child which is ill. This means the mum takes time away to care for her child, missing out on her own education, and the cycle continues.

Evaluation

Both Winnie and David Hardman were shocked and angered when the cleaning contract tender was rejected. Winnie had felt sure that the Methodist canon – reaching out to those in need – would ensure that the new cleaning company would win the contract. However, as is the case with so many organisations, money is the chief concern.

Blanca

This is Blanca's story. It concerns the emotional and coercive control she has suffered at the hands of her ex-partner, the father of her youngest child. She has an older child back home in Latin America. He was being cared for by her mother, but she died suddenly six months before this interview. Blanca had no money to fly home for the funeral and worries about what is happening to her eldest son. He is now in the care of other family members. Her story highlights the dangerous position she was placed in when asked for original documentation to meet Home Office criteria when attempting to gain a visa. English is not Blanca's first language, and this is problematic when dealing with those in authority and Universal Credit.

─────────────── **Blanca's Story** ───────────────

He [former partner] put the cameras in the house. Living room, corridor, bathroom everywhere. So, I called the police again and said 'Ok, this is what it means to control.' But he says he wants to be safe. He says 'She's a liar, she lies. I want to just protect you with the camera.' This is not protection; he is not healthy mentally. He puts them here because he wants to control my life. He is watching me every minute. That is abuse for me. He is there watching me every time; on the phone, watching with maybe others and for me it is not nice. So, police tell him to leave the house.

He was gone for one year and I was alone in the house with my child, but after that he came back, oh, strong with POWER. He still keeps calling me a liar. He calls the police and tells them I spit in his face and that he wants them to take me out of **his** house. It was not true. He wanted me out of the house so he could bring his new wife from Africa. He said he was not married, he was not nervous, he did not cry, he was normal. He said to the police 'this lady is a liar, she is very nervous, she is really crazy.' I was crying, I was nervous.

One day, he went into the kitchen and took the £200 I had in my bag. He tells me I am crazy, that I have lost the money, or I did not have the money and he was just looking for a letter from the council to prove this was **his** house. Every week he gave me £40 for food and every week I kept £20 back to help me get my documents. I did not have the documents to stay in this country and this was why he kept getting the police. I was shaking in case the police came and took me back to my country. The police were good and say, 'We will not take you; your child is British.' My baby was only three years old, but I had to leave the house. I was not safe.

I found out about Winnie when I went to the Health Visitor. She wrote about how I cry and how I don't have enough food or money to pay for light [electricity]. I just told her that I didn't know what to do about it or about my child in my own country and she told me about here. She gave me the address for this church, and to come every Wednesday. I came here three years ago. Everyone here was so happy and good.

I had to get help with getting a letter to the Home Office so I could get my documents. Here they support me; they gave me help to get a temporary visa. They help me a lot. Janet [the minister at BCH] writes good things about me to the Home Office. But the Home Office, they want the original documents for my baby, and I do not have them, and I would be at risk if I went to the house to get them, so I cannot do that. Janet writes and tells them not to put me at risk with him and violence. She tells them I will send copies and that copies are enough to prove my child is British. But Home Office did not want copies, they wanted all the originals. Janet was praying and she supported me until Home Office said OK. I got my visa.

Evaluation

Blanca works part-time, as a cleaner, on a zero hours contract. She works unsociable hours. She has to wake her daughter every morning and take her to a childminder before going to work. They do not get back home until very late. She has problems filling in the Universal Credit forms as she has limited access to the internet and, when she does get online, her English is not of a standard that will enable her to complete the forms without help. At the time of writing, Blanca has not had childminding money refunded to her. She is struggling to pay her bills and buy food. She fears she can no longer afford to work. If she stops working, she will be deemed to have made herself redundant and will be sanctioned. That Blanca is trapped in a low paid job correlates with the research findings of Tracy Shildrick where she notes, participants 'were trapped in what is often described as a low-pay, no-pay cycle not by choice but because of the opportunities they were faced with in their local labour markets' (Shildrick 2018, p.6). Blanca does not choose to work such unsociable hours; it is the only job open to her. Throughout all of her struggles with the system, Blanca continues to have faith. The following is a WhatsApp message posted to the group as she struggled to get her childcare money refunded:

> Thank you, Winnie, God is with us. I am sad no pay [*sic.*] to my Universal account, no body answers my calls. But I believe in God, definitely things will change. (Blanca 2020)

Coercive control is a gendered act of domestic violence where women are almost always the victim. This, as Robinson and colleagues point out, it 'can be explained to a large degree by women's continued default status as responsible primarily for domestic and caring work' (Robinson et al. 2018, p.31). It has recently been deemed a criminal act in England and Wales, however research has shown that there is a 'spectrum of understanding' with those working in statutory agencies when it comes to the new law (Robinson et al. 2018)). This lack of understanding is apparent in Blanca's story. Although the police asked her ex-partner to leave the house during the first incident, it is Blanca and her young daughter who are eventually forced into homelessness. The Home Office – the department not only responsible for immigration matters but also for law and order – also shows a lack of understanding of the dangers Blanca faces.

Martha

This is Martha's experience of Universal Credit and the problems she has with it being paid in arrears. She is a single mum with three young children and works part time for a local council. These are Martha's own words transcribed from a group session at Mummies Republic. Martha's problems with the assessment period have been documented in the introductory chapter.

Martha's Story

My issue is with the childcare and the assessment period. Universal Credit is not benefiting me. I'm worse off each month. It looks like I earn £3000. If I earn that I wouldn't be eligible for Universal Credit. I asked If there is a way that my system can be changed so that it can factor in that when I get paid early on a Friday when my normal pay day falls on a weekend. Or the dates fall out of the normal assessment period, like at Christmas, can we try to change it? They were like, 'No, we are not allowed. No, that's it. We can't do it; we can't shut it down.' They told me to sort it out with my employers, ask them to pay me the Monday after, instead of the Friday before. I asked but they cannot do that. I work for the council as well, it's like

I work for the government and if they cannot sort it who can? I am the one who loses out.

So, for one month I will, for that month, get nothing. It will say zero. So, I still got the childcare payments to pay and I have to pay up front. Yes, I get it back the following month but for that month, I'm left with nothing because I've got to pay childcare and I got no money form Universal Credit. Now, with the childcare, Universal Credit tell me it's my employers' fault because they're not feeding the live feed. Again, I am the one who loses out.

And I said, 'Well, my employers aren't gonna change the date to suit Universal Credit, you know, because it's been that way for God knows how long, before Universal Credit came along. The system should recognise that, "Oh, okay, she gets paid the 20th of every month but this day it came a bit forward because the 20th fell on a weekend."' It doesn't work like that though. They're not willing to help, they're not willing to change, they're not willing to do anything here because anytime that happens, and that happens twice a year, I'm at a disadvantage. I fall in big-time arrears; I get pressured from the childcare because they need to pay for their staff. They're looking after my kids. So, what do I do? Because childcare is like a mortgage, you need to pay it. It's not something like £40 that is affordable. I can go for an advance, but an advance is not enough to help pay the monthly childcare, and I have to pay it back. What do I do? I'm in arrears, the childcare is breathing down my neck saying that, 'Well, we need the money. When are you gonna get the money?' And I'm telling them that it's not me. It's because of the assessment period, they're penalising me.

My employers are blaming Universal Credit, Universal Credit are blaming my employers, and that has made me, and the kids, lose out. If they decide not to look after my child due to non-payment, I'm out of work. So, if I'm out of work then that means I've intentionally made myself out of work due to their system, a system that doesn't work. It's a loss–loss for me. The government are saying they're helping with Universal Credit to help people get back into work, but if you can't fix the system, for the system to recognise that for that month the 20th fell on a weekend then the system isn't working. I can't help those guys with the IT system. Those guys need to sort it out.

With the childcare credit, it says up to 85%. Well, that's not true because if the childcare is at £1000, then I'd be paying £150 but they capped it at £664 for one child and for two children is £1164. So how do you pay up to 85% worth of childcare costs? You know, that's misleading. It's discrimination because London has been capped at that but if you go up to Newcastle, then you'll get up to the 85%, because childcare is cheaper up there. Then it's not universal.

Evaluation

Martha remains angry with the way in which the payments for childcare are paid in arrears. She has to find the money to pay the nursery school no matter what is happening with her Universal Credit payments. If the system perceives she is being paid twice in a month, for that month she gets nothing. Universal Credit also caps the amount it gives for childcare. With prices in London being much higher than the rest of the UK, no one in London gets 85% refunded. Martha argues that for it to be 'Universal', 85% should be across the entire country and take into account the differing costs faced by families in need in relation to where they are residing.

The following chapter examines the problems many of the women have with mental health. The stress of fighting the system just to get what is owed to them takes its toll. Group support, both giving and receiving, is important to all of the group. Things changed as I wrote these three chapters as the coronavirus pandemic forced the country into lockdown. As the lockdown came into effect, and weeks became months, the women were forced to support each other through WhatsApp messages and Zoom calls. We began a blog and the women and older children were encouraged to put their feelings into words.

CHAPTER 5

Mental Health

Helping others, helping ourselves

This chapter will begin by examining the ways in which Mummies Republic has helped the women with mental health issues. They work closely with a psychologist and have 'Talking Therapy' sessions with a team from the Maudsley Hospital in London.[22] This team and other mental health support teams have discovered that they have better attendance and results if they go to the community group as opposed to the group going to a hospital setting. Ella Darbyshire works with different community groups in North London and helps with a women's session at a local mosque:

> We have found that we get much better participation and a larger uptake for our services if we visit the mosque. This is a safe space for the women. There is a real feeling of stigma surrounding mental health issues within this demographic and they would not seek professional help on their own. We go to them and there is no stigma. (Ella Darbyshire 2020)

That many of the women were experiencing mental health problems was apparent to Winnie from the start. She has worked tirelessly to put the necessary help in place. Not all

---

22 Sadly, due to the coronavirus pandemic, the Talking Therapy sessions had to stop. They had hoped to do these weekly by Zoom video conferencing but with limited staff this was not possible.

of this help comes from external agencies and the benefits of giving and receiving support and help from within the group are examined in this chapter.

Winnie

Our work with the mental health team has been progressive. This was enabled by a mental health practitioner visiting one of our meetings. We at Mummies Republic saw the potential of what was on offer as our constituents experience stress. We now receive group CBT sessions. One benefit is that it is quicker for women to access an appointment to other mental health services through this session than through a doctor. The local mental health team also signpost women to Mummies Republic.

It is through our Talking Therapy sessions that we began to acknowledge the benefits of withdrawing from the stressful environment as a way to enable resilience. Since then, every year, we have sought to facilitate retreats to Butlins Holiday Park for the families. One of our clients, a survivor of child sexual abuse, greatly benefits from these retreats. Getting away from the stresses of everyday life in London and spending time with other women removes the feelings of isolation and helps with anxiety. The retreat is used as a drug-free intervention.

Health visitors also refer women to us as socioeconomic factors prevent those on the edge of society from accessing play groups. Low confidence and poor judgement all play a part in placing people outside social groups and situations. The health visitors tell us that Mummies Republic is the safest of environments for them. One mum was referred to us on the basis that she had postnatal depression. She did not engage with any statutory systems. In a disclosure to me, as the third sector, she spoke of the possibility she may have been trafficked. Many people would find it difficult to believe that someone would not know if they had been trafficked or not. This mum was unaware as, it appeared, that her move to London was organised as a favour. It was carried out by a friend of a friend, or so she was told, to help her get out of a very bad situation in her home country.

On signposting her to the mental health team, she was diagnosed with postnatal psychosis. This may have been compounded by the trafficking situation as she was the victim of sexual abuse by those who were meant to be helping her. On engaging with Mummies Republic, she gained enough trust to engage with mental health services. One day she rang me from the hospital. She was distressed and revealed that she was surrounded by about seven people including her potential abuser. It was chaotic and she was extremely anxious and upset.

It was only on my arrival, with the Housing and Welfare officer, did she open up, something the practitioners were struggling to get her to do. The doctor in charge arrived and her rudeness led to an eruption from the Housing and Welfare officer. They were so angry at the way in which the doctor spoke to the mum and to us. In the end we were all asked to leave. The mum was the obvious loser in this case and that was when I realised that a formal relationship with the NHS was necessary. This is currently being perused by the Southwark and Maudsley NHS team where I will have recognition as an honorary Member of the NHS – but, like all things that involve bureaucracy, it is taking time. (Winnie 2019)

Evaluation
Human trafficking is a problem in the UK, the scale of which has only recently been acknowledged. Media coverage, along with policy and political debate, appear to confirm that slavery is indeed an alarming contemporary global phenomenon (Craig et al. 2019). Many people trafficked into the country are forced to work in industries such as agriculture, construction, car washes and nail bars. Many women and young girls are forced into the sex trade (antislavery.org). It may seem odd to others in our society that someone does not recognize that they have been trafficked:

> Typically, a person coming from a situation of poverty and lack of opportunity gets an offer of an apparently

good job in the UK. Often the victim has to take a loan from an agent to pay for the recruitment fees and for the journey. (antislavery.org/slavery-today/slavery-uk/)

The trafficker in this story was able to attend the hospital without fear of being accused of trafficking and coercion. There are many reasons as to why they could be so sure of not being exposed. This mum may have felt fear through intimidation, fear of not being believed or it may be that she had nowhere else to go, no one else to turn to when discharged from hospital:

> The UK government's deliberate creation of an environment that is hostile to 'illegal workers' is one example of how, while rightly declaring outrage at those who abuse and enslave others, the UK has created a space in which criminals can more easily exploit people with insecure immigration status. (Roberts 2019, p.151)

This woman was given emergency safe accommodation but despite this, and the support she was given by social services and Mummies Republic, she vanished. This is not an unusual scenario for those who have been rescued from a trafficked/slavery situation. Those who have been 'rescued' from modern day slavery receive forty-five days of help, accommodation and support from the UK government. This seems a woefully short period of intervention for those who are vulnerable and have no other support network in the U.K. A governmental report highlights the lack of follow up data once the forty-five days are over:

> There has been no extensive research conducted, nor data obtained, to analyse and assess what happens to victims of human trafficking following the support they receive during the statutory 45-day period...Little is known as to what happens to victims of slavery and trafficking once they leave the safe house, or support

ends following a Conclusive Grounds decision, and even less is known of those who have no support or benefits. No data is collected on long term outcomes for victims. (publications.parliament.uk)[23]

Not only do they have no other means of support, many fear being deported back to their home countries:

Typically, young men and women from poorer parts of the world enter the United Kingdom with the expectation of seeking paid work, returning wages to their families. When they get placed in care for their own protection some escape, either because they are aware of their family's debt (ECPAT 2011) or because they feel indebted to those who have assisted their travel and resettlement. (Gadd and Broad 2018, p.1460).

Kelly

Kelly is a single mum with two young daughters. They live in a tower block, similar in build to Grenfell Tower. Her eldest daughter, aged eleven, has been particularly affected by the Grenfell Tower fire and worries they are in danger. Kelly is afraid her daughter takes on board too many of her own fears and concerns. All the children are given opportunities to speak about their anxieties and, during a retreat camp, art was used to initiate discussions. It was during one such session that her daughter raised her fear of a Grenfell Tower disaster befalling their own tower block.

─────────────── **Kelly's Story** ───────────────

The major thing is support. It's not just the one day a week thing, if that makes sense? It's not just the Wednesday. I know if I message

---

23 See https://publications.parliament.uk/pa/cm201617/cmselect/
    cmworpen/803/80305.htm for full report.

Winnie or call Winnie, even if I'm not asking for help, she'll always give me support, doing what she can through Mummies Republic.

I didn't know the other ladies for very long when, at a meeting, I just teared up and had a cry. The group makes you feel safe, safe enough to do that. That's the major thing I get from it. Just having support helps a lot. My own family are near but it's a very different relationship I have with my family to everyone else in my life. I suffer with depression and anxiety, but they don't really know half of it because I don't feel like I can talk to them about it. Whereas, complete strangers I'm quite open, weirdly, I don't know why.

I think if I didn't have the kids, I'd be a mess. I've got to get up for them. I tend to have my life in stages. I have to get up because they've got to go to school. While I'm ironing their uniforms, I'll iron my work uniform, then it's time for school. When I've dropped them at school, I'll get the bus to the tube station. Once I'm at the tube station, I'll then get the tube to work. I have to do everything in little bits, which is weird to some people but that's just how I just have to do each day. Mummies Republic gives me a sense of, 'It's okay to do that. It's okay.' Just being able to talk, even if it's just mundane things, it's still having that conversation, an adult conversation, it helps.

I tend to put myself with the kids, I can do that. I can be mum, but it's Kelly who I struggle to be. As long as I'm being mum or being with kids in general, I'm quite good at that and then I struggle being me on my own. Just being an adult, just being a person, me. Mummies Republic is another outlet. Just being amongst people, and most of the time you find you are not just the only one. What also helps is the advice you get. Someone's been in the same situation, they can guide you from their experience and that helps.

I do class myself as being religious, but I don't pray often and don't know Bible quotes and things. I am very aware that there is a God but unlike many others I can't find peace with it and just put my life in his hands. I do pray sometimes but then I feel guilty for just doing it then and not all the time. I should be praying all the time and being a better person. See, I always find a way to kick myself. (Kelly)

Evaluation

The support Kelly has been given has seen her grow in confidence. Kelly would not have agreed to give her story a year ago. She is not on Universal Credit but, having heard the stories from those already on the system, she has concerns as to the affects it may have on her and her daughters. Throughout the WhatsApp chats Kelly was the only one never to mention prayer or religion. However, religion is important to her. Although she does not attend church, she spoke of wanting to go to her local church, which is Anglican, but feared that the girls would fidget or get bored and that others would judge her for that.

Laura

Laura, a single mum with three boys, has played a major role in Mummies Republic, becoming one of the central figures in the group. Laura is not, at present, on Universal Credit but remains on the old benefits system. She very much epitomises the ethos of the group – 'for mummies by mummies' – and has helped out in numerous ways. This is Laura's story, as told to me during a Wednesday meeting.

———————————— **Laura's Story** ————————————

I'm a qualified nurse. Everything was fine but I've had anorexia from the age of twelve, so I've been in and out of the Mental Health system. When I was twenty-five, I had to give up work because I made a few suicide attempts. Things got really rough. I was struggling because there are government cuts on the mental health system, so, when I need help you don't get it. You have to go on a six-months waiting list and if you do need help before that, you've got to go to A&E, a normal A&E. To be honest, it turns you off, because I've got children, they automatically say to you, 'Have you got children?' and then

Social Services get involved. I know there's stigma attached to having mental health problems and I always worry about it. It is noted on their system and I don't like the thought. So, I sort of suffer in silence and I find it hard to cope.

I was going through a really tough time when I lost my purse. I didn't know what to do, I phoned the Job Centre, they said come to the BCH, because it was a Friday and there was a foodbank. That was when Winnie saw me. She could just see that I wasn't quite right. I was having one of my really bad episodes. She went up to the office and got me the form for Mummies Republic and told me all about it. I came the following Wednesday, and since then, this has been a lifeline. And I think that was a Divine intervention. And I think that it was meant to be that I met Winnie that day.

Everyone here is so lovely, so nice. We all chip in, all try and help out. I'd love to go back to work. If I commit to going back to work and I get ill the rent has still got to be paid and I'll get into arrears. I once ended up getting evicted from my property a week before Christmas with the kids. When you're mentally ill, you can't do the system and fill out all these forms. You can't get the help. There used to be a help center called the Chauncey Centre, you could just go there when you were struggling and they would help you, but now that's closed, there's nothing. Mummies Republic is vital, this is a life-changer for me. I look forward to Wednesdays. I come here as often as I can. I'll do as much voluntary work as I can, I like to keep myself busy. I'm not a lazy person, I've always been a worker and doing nursing. You've got a caring nature and you want to help others and helping others it what helps me.

I come in here on Wednesdays. Help cook, help set up the stuff for the kids. Thursdays, I'll be coming in to do the baby clinic. I open up the store here, do teas, coffees, cakes for the kids, play with the kids while the mums are getting a bit of a break. So yeah, I'll be doing that. Also, I've got another job, sorting clothes out because we're going to do a clothes bank. This is my lifeline and well, you know, it's brilliant. They really gave me my health back. (Laura)

Evaluation

Laura is concerned about the effects Universal Credit will have on her and her children's lives, as she has seen how detrimental it has been to friends and family. Laura pointed out, during a group discussion, that when she has a problem with her finances she wants to sit down and ask for help face to face. Universal Credit does not work that way. She will have to telephone and ask for an appointment and all of that takes time, time, when she is ill, she doesn't have. Laura fears for the future as her needs, like so many others, are not 'Universal'.

Laura's mental health issues are preventing her from undertaking paid employment but the sense of self-worth she has gained from volunteering at Mummies Republic is evidence that this group gives help in many different ways. Research has shown that becoming the provider of help can be beneficial to those who usually are receivers, 'Having the opportunity to change roles from recipient to provider may reduce the self-threat related to seeking and receiving help, and boost self-competence' (Alvarez and van Leewuwen 2015, p.3). It can enable the women to become proactive in times of crisis.

As I write this chapter, I have not seen Laura for over a year and realise she is not on the WhatsApp group that has been set up during the pandemic. I ask the group if anyone has heard from her. Martha reports that she met Laura by chance in February, just before lockdown. Laura had spoken of returning to the group, no one else has any news of her. No one has contact details for her.

On the 19th August 2020 Laura was tragically killed in an accident whilst on holiday with her children. The group was devastated by the news. Laura was an important member of the group and will be missed by us all. As one mum wrote on the WhatsApp group "she was a beautiful soul".

Holiday Time

Holidays may appear to be a luxury, something that is out of reach for these women and their children. For those of us lucky enough not to be living in poverty, going on holiday is a part of our lives. They offer a respite from the mundane; a chance to recharge and relax. Yet, for a section of society, holidays are a luxury they cannot afford. However, research has shown that taking a holiday is important for those with long term mental health issues (Pols and Kroon 2007). Winnie spoke of the advantages of taking a small group of mums and children to a Butlins Holiday Park for five days.

> One place that has lots of happy memories for the mums and the children is Butlins. As I have mentioned, this is our annual retreat, a place to feel safe, be with others in similar situations, laugh and relax. In the words of one of the mums, 'at least this year my son will have something more than "I went to the park" to report on his first day back at school.' This opportunity relieves food poverty as well as giving the parent and child their own bed to sleep in. It also widens their outlook and experiences as there is exposure to new areas other than the local SE17, SE16 radius. As it is all inclusive, there is no financial burden on mums' pockets. This also reflects both Christian discipline of retreats and mental health discipline of leaving the stressful environment. (Winnie)

Evaluation

The women were given a respite from the stress of ensuring there was enough food on the table. They had other adults to talk to in the evenings when the children were in bed. Winnie also spoke of one mum who, for the first time in many years, had a bed to call her own, no longer sharing with her child. This relates to the research carried out by Pols and Kroon into the importance of holidays for people with mental illness. They found that their participants, when on holiday as a group 'were able to talk about themselves in a positive way, without discussing problems, health care or worries….it gives them a sense of self-esteem' (Pols and Kroon 2007, p.263). One aspect that is worth noting is that, when on holiday, the women had a new identity: they were now tourists.

Sadly, these holidays are expensive and in 2019 funds were in such short supply that a week away was not achievable. In its place Winnie secured two nights at a religious retreat centre just outside London. I joined them for one day and, despite the rain, the majority were able to relax and enjoy the countryside. Not all who attended the retreat enjoyed the experience. When I arrived, on the second morning, one mum was leaving with her two children. Being away from her home environment proved too stressful. As Gao et al. point out, this is not an unusual scenario:

> Holiday trips or vacations are not always pleasant. Other researchers have come to the same conclusion. They have reported travel-related health problems such as homesickness (Kop, Vingerhoets, Kruithof, & Gottdiener 2003; Pearce 1981; Van Heck & Vingerhoets 2007; Vingerhoets, Sanders, & Kuper 1997); worrying during trips (Larsen, Brun, & Ogaard 2009); relational problems (Ryan 1991); as well as culture shock (Pearce, 1981). Hence, it is plausible that experiencing a holiday with unpleasantness or stress may lead to lower feelings of happiness. (Gao et al. 2018, p.568)

This is an important aspect to consider when evaluating the benefits of removing individuals from a perceived stressful environment.

The mental health benefits Mummies Republic has for the women is evident. From Talking Therapy sessions to holidays, from being supported to giving support. Martha summed up the culture of the group: 'What makes mummies different is that no one ever judges. Not many groups can say that' (Martha 2020).

CHAPTER 6

Lockdown

Our Thoughts

Initially this chapter was to be co-written by the women. It was decided that we would undertake this task as a cooperative, using Wednesday evening sessions to gather ideas and write. I decided the most advantageous time to do this would be springtime. The nights are lighter, the weather less inclement and therefore the probabilities of getting more women to attend was higher than during the dark winter evenings.

In March 2020, with the pandemic taking hold, the UK went into lockdown and plans changed. Winnie had set up a WhatsApp group to enable the women to continue to support each other. She also organized Zoom meetings as a way of 'seeing' everyone; the fear of isolation was on our minds. It was also decided that we set up a blog to give the women a voice. This gave them a platform to let the wider population realise what life is like living in London, in a low-income family with, for some, little or no outdoor space. Some lost their jobs, some were furloughed, some worked from home and others discovered they were an essential part of the frontline workforce. Some became COVID-19 positive and others watched family members become ill. Sadly, some were bereaved. There were brighter times, times for celebration. A new grandson was welcomed into the world, children had birthday celebrations, and, during Zoom meetings, we laughed. The blog and the WhatsApp messages are now their co-written chapter. Their lives in lockdown.

Prayer

The importance of religion to these women was never more apparent than during the pandemic. The WhatsApp messages are full of prayers, biblical passages, videos of gospel singers and praying hands emojis. The following prayers were posted after Winnie asked the group for prayers for herself, and me, as we both had family members in ICU with COVID-19:

> Good morning Winnie and Miss Yvonne may the comfort of God help you in this difficult time and do not be afraid. Stand firm and you will see deliverance in Jesus name. (Prudence, April 2020)

> Dear loving Lord,

> As Yvonne's dad and family goes through this difficult time, please make their time less painful and show them the way that in darkness, you are the light that will never burn out! In Jesus's name, your will be done 🙏🙏🙏 x (Martha, April 2020)

Very few of the women attend church on a regular basis. Organised religion is not a feature for the majority and their children. Yet, prayer remains their sacred canopy in times of need. This resonates with Crawford-Sullivan as, during her research she observed how:

> prayer and religious beliefs played a defining role in their daily lives, although organized religion often played little or no part. (Crawford-Sullivan 2011, p.3).

Interestingly, the prayers used in the WhatsApp group are a mixture of conversational prayer alongside quotes from the Scriptures. These were used as a means of connecting with God and off offering support to others in the group. These prayers were all that could be offered up during the lockdown as a means of showing solidarity and support. This reverberates with Day's suggestion that, for the women in her research, 'prayer was about talking to God about God-given matters' (Day 2017, p.101).

The following messages explain the importance of prayer to this group of London mothers.

> Morning Yvonne! Prayers is really important to me as it is a way just to talk to God and feel reassured about certain things that are unsettling me and know that... one I am forgiven; two he fights my battles and three I am at peace with my Lord. (Martha, May 2020)

> Prayer is important because it makes us more like Jesus and because it reveals to us the heart and mind of God.

> "And pray in the Spirit on all occasions with all kinds of prayers and requests. With this in mind, be alert and always keep on praying for all the Lord's people." (Ephesians 6:18) (Janina, May 2020)

Formal religion is not what matters to the women of Mummies Republic. Rather, having God and religion be a part of their everyday lives through prayer and scripture supports the women and their families, a support they share with all the group. It is 'a form of emotional labour' (Day 2017, p.103), an extension of the gendered nurturing role allocated to mothers (Crawford-Sullivan 2011; Day 2017).

Our Blog

The importance of being heard was discussed in the previous chapter. During lockdown, where many of the women were alone with their children, the need to be acknowledged was ever more apparent. The following extracts are taken from the blog. We decided to use some of the children's stories as they had started to draw and write as a means of expressing their feelings.

Birthday Celebrations, April 11th

Lucca (two years old) was at home with me, his sister and daddy. I had planned to do a big party with Mummies Republic on Wednesday. I had been planning this during the whole year. It should have had a theme of superhero. He loves Captain America, but, unfortunately, we could not do it. I just bought a little cake and we celebrated at home. We had a lovely time. All of the Mummies Republic sent Happy Birthday messages on WhatsApp. (Janina)

Easter Monday Reflections, April 14th

The stillness of the streets during COVID-19 brought a sense of nostalgia from my childhood; where Good Friday and Easter Monday were closed to all trading. Family was brought together, and consumerism quietened. If you had forgotten to buy something, well tough luck!

Church on Friday? That was always my thought regarding Good Friday. If it was so good, why are we wearing black? Why are the scripture readings so intense? The eerie sounds of Handel's *Messiah* 'Behold the Lamb of God' my lasting memory of the morning's service, now fused with Franco Zeffirelli's afternoon matinee *Jesus of Nazareth*. For lunch I continue and wonder why are we forced to eat fish? Naturally, I look forward to Easter Day, when we feast on that New Zealand lamb wrapped in mint and thyme.

Unlike my nostalgia, Church buildings too are closed. Loved ones isolated. Some people question what good will come out of lockdown? Government COVID-19 updates inform of the growing death toll. Europe as the current epicentre of COVID-19 wears a black veil. This is, in practice, an extended Good Friday.

The communal experience of witnessing sacrificial acts of service by the frontline, lives saved, lives lost, lives in isolation and lives in poverty must serve as the memory and gratitude to the ones gone before us and to the ones that serve us.

The old ways of undermining our cleaners, carers and shop assistants must be done with. Our extended Good Friday experience informs us that they are as socially valuable as our medical practitioners. We must therefore change the way we live.

The NHS fights for every life, so too must we fight to recognise every life as equal. Equitable healthcare, equitable housing, equitable education, equitable employment and equitable income. That is the Good in the message of Easter, we are all equal and through the actions of love been given a second chance at life. (Winnie)

Frontline Mummy, April 15th

I am a very proud single mum to two beautiful girls aged eight and eleven. This COVID-19 outbreak and lockdown, as you can imagine, for me and many other families has been a very worrying time. I've worked for a supermarket chain now for the past twenty years and never believed myself to be an important part of society by doing this job but, during this time of crisis, I am classed as a keyworker. I am able to leave the house to attend work and my children have been given a place at school so I can resume my job to help supply the nation with food. It makes me proud to know that I'm doing my bit, but I am also in fear because it puts me and my children at a higher risk. Having to leave the house so often makes me very anxious. Being a single parent makes this situation even harder because being the sole earner in my household and having to support two children, if I don't go to work, I have no income to cover bills, etc. That thought does not bear thinking about. I'm very lucky that my children are able to attend school and they enjoy it which is a big relief. I feel guilty every day I have to drop them there. I'm doing all I can personally to keep me and my kids as safe as we can when not in the house. While trying to shield them as much as I can but also making sure they understand the seriousness of the situation. There is a really fine balance. (Kelly)

Martha's Week, April 17th

What a week! I have learnt that two people that I work with had passed away due to the virus and a family member has also passed. This has broken my heart and I am ever so sad and tearful at times as, during this difficult time, family and friends cannot be together for one and other. On the other hand, my neighbour's partner passed away four weeks ago. He had cancer and, this Tuesday, he made his final journey. From my front door, as the hearse came to my block, I was able to say goodbye to the most lovely, humble man that I had a pleasure of knowing. From a distance, I was glad to be there for my wonderful neighbour as she said goodbye to her loved one. Each day I am thanking God for allowing me and my family see another day. As a single mum of three young children (eight and three and a five-month-old) my mothering skills have really been challenged during this lockdown. In a space of a month I have tried to become a teacher, a chef, a cleaner, an accountant, and most importantly a mum, day after day. Doing this constantly has made me lose my mind, and patience and I am continually tired. On many days, I don't know what day it is… let alone what year we are in. I knew being a mum was hard but never this hard during such a difficult time. I have some grace during the week as I am listed down as a key worker and my eldest gets to go to school. I am thankful to the school as this gives me some respite and peace. I'm trying to stay strong for my children as they don't really understand what the world is having to do battle with. There are so many people dying. My eldest child keeps asking questions about this pandemic and I am often sad that I have no definitive answer as to when this will be over. I do keep telling them we should be thankful to God and the NHS as they are doing their best to keep all of us alive, including themselves. This lockdown has bought so many challenges, emotions and new skills, I am somewhat losing myself and in the same breath, learning something new within myself. Spending more time with the kids has shown me how quickly they have grown. I am finding I am getting to know and understand my children's characters and what they like doing. A lot of the time they are at school/nursery, and staff are telling me how they are doing and what areas they enjoy learning. Now I get to see that for myself. One thing I am thankful for is time, it has allowed me to be reconnected to God. As I watch what the world is going through, I have been able to lean to God to give me strength and not be afraid. As Dolly Parton said… when this shall pass, we as a nation will become better people! (Martha)

The Cruellest Virus, April 21st
Yesterday we were all saddened to hear that one of our group has lost their brother to COVID-19. Only last week he was showing signs of a recovery, sadly it did not last, and he passed away. A young man taken too soon from his family.

We cannot begin to imagine her grief nor that of her family when they could not get to say their goodbyes or be with him as he died. We can only take a minute to tell her she has our thoughts and prayers through our WhatsApp group. It in no way comes close to holding her but it is the best we have.

This aspect, of isolation, of being apart at times of greatest need is what makes this virus so cruel. (Yvonne)

Doreen's Approach to the News, April 23rd
I stopped putting on the news for my kids. For the past two weeks even, I haven't watched the news. I was finding it quite depressing. If I am going to watch the news, I will watch it on my phone. I don't want the kids to be watching it. They have been coping with the lockdown, but I worry about them. Since school closed, they don't really want to go out. They have been out only four times to the park. Any time I go out shopping they are always praying for me. My second oldest is going to be sixteen years old she has hasn't been out at all. She doesn't want to; she doesn't feel safe. (Doreen)

Bea: An Award-Winning Author, April 27th
Bea is 10 years old and is Lucca's sister. The family is originally from Brazil. Bea has started writing a book/diary. Books are her passion. Last year she won a Mary Seacole award for creative

writing. At Mummies Republic sessions, Bea can always be found either helping with the younger children or sitting with her nose in a book.

Dear best friend, I hope you are good, generally good. Since you've been gone it has not been easy. I want to say, 'thank you'. Even though it broke me into a million pieces when you left, I want to say, 'thank you'. Even though I miss you every day, thank you for inspiring me. Inspiring me to face my fears. You make me want to be better. You make me want to work on myself, and even though doing this without you by myside is one of the hardest things I ever had to do, but I'm doing it.

Bea.

The Reality of Working from Home and being Mummy, April 28th

Since the lockdown started, I have been working from home and, at the same time, looking after my six-year-old son. It has not been easy for me especially when I have to deal with a six-year-old full of energy who does not understand the situation we are living in at the moment. He does not understand why he has to stay indoors and is not allowed outside to play. He was frustrated from the start and I felt so sorry for him because of not having space to play and not even a balcony to go out onto for fresh air. I just keep explaining again and again and, as the days have gone past, he has started to understand it a little bit better.

The lockdown is really getting to me because I am working Monday–Friday and on top of that I have to assist my son with his schoolwork, which is sent to him every day from his teacher.

It feels like I have not got a life anymore. I am just hoping and praying for this situation to come to end so that people can go back to live their normal life as before. May God take control. (Prudence)

The Wildlife is Taking Over the World, April 29th

The news has been full of kangaroos jumping down the main streets of Australia, a racoon walking through Central Park in New York and a herd of goats on the streets of Wales. Blanca has her own wildlife story. A pigeon has decided to visit her most days, coming in through the window, and is quite at home sitting on the back of the sofa.

Photograph taken by Blanca

Here are some of the WhatsApp messages about the bird. It has brought Blanca a lot of joy.

Nana: Blanca, they say it's a good sign and good thing will happen to you soon 🙏🙏🙏 and as you are saying it's twice the price so enjoy.

Blanca: I know God protects my house. I am happy God sent an angel to me. I see the bird two times. She has eggs in a nest outside my house. I will take photos of the eggs

I believe, everyone, that God love me such much. Am happy today. I believe she is from an angle because she has three colours, beautiful.

Lynsey: I believe it is angel too [*sic*], God always finds a way to comfort us, we are so lucky to have such an amazing father by our side always.

WhatsApp Group

Our Life in Lockdown, May 1st

Today's blog is by Chloe and her sister Rebecca. Chloe is eleven and Rebecca eight. Their mum is a frontline worker, so the girls go to school four days a week.

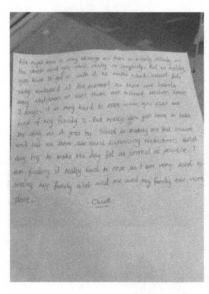

Life right now is very strange there is nearly nobody on the streets and you can't really see anybody. But in reality, you have to get on with it no matter what. School feels very awkward at the moment as there are barely any children in and there are different teachers every two days. It is very hard to cope when you can't see most of my family. But really you just have to take the day as it goes by. School is making me feel secure and safe as there are social distancing restrictions and they try to make the day feel as normal as possible. I am finding it really hard to cope as I am very used to seeing my family a lot and me and my family are very close.

Chloe

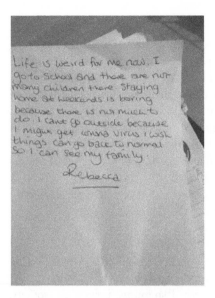

Life is weird for me now. I go to school and there are not many children there. Staying home at weekends is boring because there is not much to do. I can't go outside because I might get corona virus. I wish things can go back to normal so I can see my family.

Rebecca

Another Problem, May 4th

The lockdown does not stop the day to day problems we are experiencing. Over the past few days one of our group has been having problems with Universal Credit repayments. English is not her first language and filling out the forms online is difficult, as is speaking on the telephone to advisors.

Today we learn that another mum has had her house flooded due to a leaking hot water tank. Not only does she now have to clear up the damage, but the family has no hot water. The council has been out to survey the damage but cannot say when repairs will be carried out.

Throughout all the problems and heartache, Mummies Republic stands by its motto:

for mummies by mummies (Yvonne)

The Power of Prayer, May 14th

Yvonne, prayer 🙏 is very important to me it makes us more like Jesus and because it reveals to us the heart and mind of

God, my children they pray every night they cannot go to bed without praying I am encouraging them to pray in the morning since the lockdown I find peace in my heart when I pray makes me feel close to God and fasting

'Do not be anxious about anything, but in everything, by prayer and petition, with thanksgiving, present your requests to God, which transcends all understanding, will guard your hearts and your minds in Christ Jesus.' (Philippians 4:6–7)

'Pray in the spirit on all occasions with all kinds of prayers and requests.' (Ephesians 6:18)

With this in mind, be alert and always keep on praying for all the Lord's people. Amen 🙏 (Doreen)

One Week Later, May 17th

It is a week since Boris gave us the new guidelines for the easing of lockdown. So, what has changed? How do we feel?

The schools are a concern. Two mums, as frontline workers, have had their children at school throughout the lockdown. For them nothing changes. One of the other mums has a son in Year 6, due to return to school. For all of the others nothing is changing.

The concern is that Mummies Republic mums mostly live in Southwark, an area with a high BAME population. A population, as we now know is more at risk from coronavirus. It is one of the worst hit areas in the country. It is important that the children return to school for their wellbeing and their education, but will suitable provisions be put in place? If there is a spike will this affecting the full opening of schools in September? The feeling is that London should be the last area to be reopening schools and Southwark the last borough in London to open its doors.

When it comes to going back to work here are some observations:

We haven't changed anything we are doing and won't for another couple of weeks I won't let me, and my family be the guinea pigs to see if it's safe. The buses are a little busier but to be honest they started to get busier a while ago now. We have to do what right for us. (**Kelly**)

Morning everyone nothing has changed concerning the school I think I heard that its reception and Year 6 that will go back. I am still working from home I don't think I will go back soon to work because the infection and the way they are still dealing with the situation has not really changed. (**Prue**)

Same here Kelly. Deaths and new COVID cases are still happening daily, I will be staying the same and do not want my son back to school until September when hopefully a significant change has happened in regard to COVID. (**Lynsey**)

There doesn't seem to be much confusion over what is happening re relaxing the lockdown measures. The overall feeling is that we will all do what is best for us and our families. (WhatsApp Group)

Implications

We can learn

The writing of this book was motivated by Winnie Baffoe and the women of Mummies Republic. This was written to give them a voice, to allow their stories to be heard by a wider audience. To study their lived religion as they navigated their way through this latest welfare reform programme, I had to gain access to their lives. I could not have achieved this without their kindness. They were generous with their time, their stories and their support. As we undertook the authorship of this book, we did not imagine the series of events that would culminate in a nationwide lockdown. We did not set out to start a blog, we had never heard of Zoom meetings, yet both became a cornerstone in this project.

The Churches are in crisis, attendance at formal worship is in decline yet, for this group of women, religion remains important. It is at the core of family life and is the foundation of support. Religion, for these women, is a lived experience. The Church has reached out to offer assistance and help them come together in solidarity as they experience hardship through welfare reform. That, not all have a religious faith, is off no consequence. Prayer is of importance and becomes the weapon of choice when supporting others in times of need. Few of the women attend formal worship, yet all weave religion into their children's lives through prayer and Wednesday Brigade.

Many of the mothers work part-time yet still find themselves struggling financially. Universal Credit has bought many challenges, caused by the dependence the system has on technology and its "Computer says no" mentality. Those in power seem unwilling to accept and fix the flaws in the system. This group had decided to take a proactive approach when it came to their problems with Universal Credit. They sat in the Palace of Westminster and watched as actors told their stories. They stood tall and answered questions, about their experiences, from the politicians. Sadly, due to the divisions brought about by Brexit, the play did not reach as many as they had hoped for.

Foodbanks need not exist, that we, as a first world country, cannot feed our children is a national embarrassment. That those who are most in need are portrayed as work-shy, 'othered' and stigmatised is a stain on our national conscious. Chris, the manager of the BCH foodbank, had this to say:

> People talk of feeling shame all the time. No one wants to use a foodbank. It is a place of last resort. I wish to see a time when foodbanks are no longer needed. (Chris 2020)

Food poverty affects both the physical and the mental wellbeing of individuals. It is a stigma and shame that is experienced, not only by the adults, but by the children. Welfare is a safety net that should ensure all are protected from hunger. This latest welfare reform programme appears to have cut holes in the net.

The women were open with their stories. Their desire was for the wider public to have an understanding of what life is like, living and working, in a low-income household. The pandemic and nationwide lockdown further isolated the women. Yet, with WhatsApp and video conferencing we managed to stay in contact. Winnie and I both needed the support of the group as we experienced close family members succumb to COVID-19. Their prayers and messages were gratefully received. The children wrote and drew pictures for the blog, and we all celebrated their birthdays. In a strange way the group became closer in isolation, remaining safe and strong in lockdown.

This book has practical implications for both the Churches and the politicians. The Churches must be open to all who cross their doors. Kelly did not attend Church due to concerns her parenting skills would be questioned. This concern may be unwarranted, but the Churches must examine the ways in which they are portraying themselves to their wider communities. They must become all inclusive, a safe space where no one would feel unwelcome no matter their situation. The must place themselves at the heart of community wellbeing and cohesion. The politicians must listen to those receiving Universal Credit. Those who have been placed on this benefit system know the problems that exist in this latest welfare reform programme. It is the clients not the civil servants who have acquired the knowledge necessary to fix the benefit system. It is only by listening to those who are in need, those who are suffering unnecessarily can we start to end the national shame that is poverty.

We must all listen to Winnie, Martha, Lynsey, Prue, Auntie P, Nivin, Laura, Kelly, Doreen, Janina and Blanca. Those in authority, in the Churches and Westminster, have a lot to learn from Mummies Republic.

"Guardian angels up above, please protect the ones we love"

Laura Perry
(1982 – 2020)

In dedicating this book to Laura Perry (1982 – 2020), she is representative of the many women and mothers who have been let down by the people and institutions which ought to maintain their human dignity.

"Guardian angels up above, please protect the ones we love" – the inscription on a gift I received from Laura. It was her expression of gratitude at the grace she received from Foodbank and Mummies Republic. Who knew that these words would be prophetic? That she would soon form a part of the legion of angels?

The inspiration for this inscription comes from 2 kings 6 :15-17, referencing a dual between with between earthly and heavenly powers. It reads:

¹⁵ When the servant of the man of God got up and went out early the next morning, an army with horses and chariots had surrounded the city. "Oh no, my lord! What shall we do?" the servant asked.

¹⁶ "Don't be afraid," the prophet answered. "Those who are with us are more than those who are with them."

¹⁷ And Elisha prayed, "Open his eyes, Lord, so that he may see." Then the Lord opened the servant's eyes, and he looked and saw the hills full of horses and chariots of fire all around Elisha.

This text reflects the situation of mothers and their children caught within the net of statutory policies and human practices which by design create harm and misery. The work of Mummies Republic is to be that prophetic presence and voice which enables hope. We serve as a conduit to the army of statutory and voluntary services which exist to enable human wellbeing, backed up by our faith in Christ Jesus.

Laura left a lasting impression on the people she met, one such impression being the love for her three sons, Charlie, Michael, and Thomas. Laura's prayer "Guardian angels up above, please protect the ones we love" has been heard and as such members of Mummies Republic have assumed that love for her boys, reflected in the funeral fund they raised to secure the wellbeing of her sons. At her funeral they lined to form a guard of honour as her casket entered the church for the last time. Laura brought people from all walks together and loved deeply. She will forever form a part of our story. (Winnie)

Appendix

Bibliography

BALDWIN, R (2011) *The Great Trade Collapse: Causes, Consequences and Prospects*. Centre for Economic Policy Research, London.

BROOKS, A (2011) *Feminist Standpoint Epistemology: Building Knowledge and Empowerment Through Women's Lived Experience*. Feminist Research practice, Sage Publications, Inc, Thousand Oaks, USA.

BROWN, C (2001) *The Death of Christian Britain*, Routledge, Oxon.

BRUCE, S (1995) *Religion in Modern Britain*, Oxford University Press, Oxford.

CHANG, H (2008) *Autoethnography as a Method,* Routledge Taylor Francis Group, London

CURRIE, DH, KELLY, DM, POMERANTZ, S (2007) "The power to squash people"; Understanding girls 'relational aggression'. British Journal of Sociological Education, Volume 28, no.1, January 2007, pp.23–27

CHILD POVERTY ACTION GROUP (2019) *Universal Credit: What You Need to Know, 5th edition.* Child Poverty Action Group, London.

DAVIE, G (1994) *Religion in Britain since 1945*, Blackwell Publishers, Oxford.

DAY A (2017) *The Religious Lives of Older Laywomen* Oxford University Press, Oxford.

DELANTY, G. (2010) *Community Second Edition*, Routledge, Taylor Francis Group, London.

EDGELL, P and DOCKA, D. (2007) Beyond the nuclear family? Familism and gender ideology in diverse religious communities. *Sociological Forum*, 22, no. 1 March 2007 pp.26–51.

GARTHWAITE, K (2016) *Hunger Pains: Life Inside Foodbank Britain*, Policy Press, University of Bristol, Bristol.

GOFFMAN, E (2009) *Stigma: Notes on the management of spoiled identity,* Simon and Schuster, New York.

HUNT, S (2005) *Religion and Everyday Life,* Routledge, Taylor and Francis Group, Oxon.

MACLEY A and KENNEDY, S (2020) *The Universal Credit assessment period and earned income* published January 9th 2020, accessed **https://researchbriefings.parliament.uk/ ResearchBriefing/Summary/CBP-8501**

MARTELA, F and RYAN, RM (2016) The Benefits of Benevolence: Basic Psychological Needs, Beneficence and the Enhancement of Wellbeing. *The Journal of Personality*, Volume 84, Issue 6, December 2016, pp.750–764.

MIN, A. K (2014) *The Deconstruction and Reconstruction of Christian Identity in a World of Difference; The Task of Theology: Leading Theologians on the Most Compelling Questions for Today,* Orbis Books, Maryknoll, New York.

MORRIS, B (1992) A Separate Violence: The Politics of Shaming. *NWSA Journal*, Vol. 4, No. 2 (Summer, 1992), pp. 200–204.

POLS, J and KROON, H (2007) The Importance of Holiday Trips for People with Chronic Mental Health Problems. *Psychiatric Services*, ps.psychiatryonline.org, February 2007, Vol. 58. No. 2.

RABINDRAKLUMAR, S (2018) retrieved from **https://www. gingerbread.org.uk/what-we-do/media-centre/single-parents-facts-figures/**

RAYNOR, R (2016) *Holding Things Together (And What Falls Apart…) Encountering and Dramatizing Austerity with Women in the North East of England* Submission for Doctor of Philosophy, Department of Geography Durham University.

ROSE, ROSENBLATT, E.L (2013) Fear and Loathing: Shame, Shaming, and Intellectual Property. *DePaul Law Review*, Volume 63, Issue 1, Fall 2013, Article 2.

ROSE J (2009) *Church on Trial.* Darton, Longman and Todd, London.

SCHREITER, R (2014) 'The Repositioning of a Theology of the World in the Face of Globalisation and Post-Secularity.' In: *The Task of Theology: Leading Theologians on the Most Compelling Questions for Today,* Orbis Books, Maryknoll, New York.

SHILDRICK, T (2018). *Poverty Propaganda: Exploring the Myths.* Policy Press, University of Bristol, Bristol.

TABRAHAM B. W (1995) *The Making of Methodism* Epworth Press, Peterborough.

WISEMAN, R (2003) *Queen Bees and Wannabes: Helping your daughter survive cliques, gossip, boyfriends and the realities of Girl World.* Little, Brown Book Group Ltd, London.

WOODHEAD, L (2011) Five concepts of religion, *International Review of Sociology*, vol.21, No.1, March 2011, pp.121–143.

CPSIA information can be obtained
at www.ICGtesting.com
Printed in the USA
BVHW031751270121
598902BV00003B/22